Beyond the March of Death

Beyond the March of Death

Memoir of a Soldier's Journey from Bataan to Nagasaki

MYRRL W. MCBRIDE, SR.

Foreword by Myrrl W. McBride, Jr.,
and Gerald F. McBride

McFarland & Company, Inc., Publishers
Jefferson, North Carolina, and London

To Elisa McBride

Library of Congress Cataloguing-in-Publication Data

McBride, Myrrl W.
   Beyond the march of death : memoir of a soldier's journey from
Batann to Nagasaki / Myrrl W. McBride, Sr. ; foreword by
Myrrl W. McBride, Jr., and Gerald F. McBride.
      p.   cm.
   Includes bibliographical references and index.

   ISBN 978-0-7864-4768-8
   softcover : 50# alkaline paper ∞

   1. McBride, Myrrl W.   2. Prisoners of war — Philippines —
Biography.   3. Prisoners of war — Japan — Biography.   4. Prisoners
of war — United States — Biography.   5. World War, 1939–1945 —
Prisoners and prisons, Japanese.   6. World War, 1939–1945 —
Personal narratives, American.   I. Title.
D805.P6M39   2010
940.54'7252092 — dc22   2010001050

British Library cataloguing data are available

Cover images ©2010 Shutterstock

Manufactured in the United States of America

McFarland & Company, Inc., Publishers
   Box 611, Jefferson, North Carolina 28640
   www.mcfarlandpub.com

Table of Contents

Foreword

by Myrrl W. McBride, Jr.,
and Gerald F. McBride

Myrrl McBride, Sr., finished typing the last pages of this book in 1948. His memories of the events were vivid and public sentiment about the war was high. The book then sat on a shelf in our home in Albuquerque, New Mexico, where he lived the last 40 years of his life. He apparently never went back to it again. It was 60 years after he typed the last page that one of us decided to send it to a publisher. After using it for a master's thesis in 1948, he never actively pursued doing anything with the book and never really spoke much about details of his war experience. When we asked questions he would often tell us to read the book. We don't know if he found it difficult to tell the detailed story more than once. It was only after his death that some of us completely read the old typed manuscript for the first time.

Over the last 60 years we have come across a few books published about Bataan. Many are documents by high-ranking officers and some are oral histories from survivors who recounted their experiences long after. It is likely that many survivors were not willing or able to write about their experience as soon as they returned. This book, however, is the story of a young, recently discharged army draftee who was still recovering from the mental and physical ordeal. As far as we know, he documented his experience as completely as he could, incorporating references where he could. These can be found in the endnotes. The narrative is all directly from the original manuscript. For the most part, his exact words were maintained, many of which are now far from being politically correct and will undoubtedly offend many readers. For this, we apologize. It was important, however, to preserve the unique voice presented here.

He was born in a very small town in western Kansas and migrated with his family as a boy to Fort Davis, Texas, after they lost almost everything during the Great Depression. After high school and a little college his sense of adventure brought him to New Mexico, and from there his life changed forever. He was the first to admit that he did not volunteer for military service. He was a young man trying to work and return to college when he was drafted from Grants, New Mexico, into a world completely foreign to him and a war he never envisioned. Soon he would endure one of the most tragic events in U.S. military history — the U.S. surrender at Bataan and the Bataan Death March. Of the 1,800 young soldiers from New Mexico who were in that notorious march, only 900 returned to the States. A year after the war ended, only 600 were still alive.

Myrrl McBride around 1941, before leaving for the Philippines.

His will to live was relentlessly challenged. The horror of the Death March was just a small part of his four years of starvation, disease and cruelty that began with the courageous stand of the 200th Coast Guard Artillery in the Battle of Bataan and continued through three and a half years as a prisoner of war in Japanese camps. His heartbreaking narrative reveals some of the qualities that undoubtedly were critical to his survival. His courage, ingenuity, sense of humor and enduring hope — all are vividly portrayed.

After his unimaginable ordeal and eventual repatriation, he went on to finish his college education, obtaining a master's degree, and became an educator himself. He taught at St. Joseph's College and worked for years with the Albuquerque public schools as a teacher, principal, and administrator. He married a high school Spanish teacher from Albuquerque named Elisa and they raised three sons. His retirement years were filled with travel, seeing cultures and places they both enjoyed. Our mother died first, and many of his last days were spent in the small cabin he built largely by himself and enjoyed immensely in the Zuni Mountains of New Mexico. He died at age 74 in his home in Albuquerque.

We all believe he passed on his spirit of mental and physical stamina and courage. All of us have gone on to test ourselves in different ways in our own lives. His victory over despair — as documented in the narrative that follows — leaves us with no boundaries to our own potential and taught us that seemingly ordinary people can do extraordinary things.

Myrrl W. McBride, Jr., and Gerald F. McBride are two of the author's three sons.

Introduction

Since the close of the Second World War, official documents relating to that event have been published in increasing numbers, and the general course of the drama has been established to the apparent satisfaction of the historians. On the personal side, too, publication of diaries, memoirs, impressions of correspondents, and similar materials has helped to reveal what the war meant in terms of individual human beings. There is danger, nevertheless, that as memory dims, and as the war recedes in time, the present generation's keen sense of war and consciousness of its meaning will also dim, and the lessons which might be learned from world catastrophe will be lost. This danger is rendered the more serious by the fact that the bulk of official documents of the war, although accurate enough, lack imaginative appeal either to those who participated in the actual events or to those who read about them in the censored dispatches from the battle fronts.

Aims of the Study

This study is the expression of a desire to do what may be possible by one person in helping to recall and preserve a sharp sense of the meaning of war. Essentially the account of one participant of World War II, it relates experiences which in a broad sense were typical. With certain incidents of the war it will hope thoroughly to familiarize the reader; these are the incidents with which the writer was personally and immediately concerned. The study will attempt to set forth the relation between these events and the reports released to the public. Finally, it will share experience, emotion, and memory with the reader in a truthful, firsthand account of war, in the hope that it will help to preserve a keen consciousness of the war as a catastrophe and thereby further a desire for universal and enduring peace.

Explanation of Terms Used

It would be absurd to attempt to picture the actual life of soldiers in action through the use of formal and academic language. Rules of grammar and proper habits of speech are forgotten or ignored by men under the pressure of battle and emergency conditions. In the following narrative an attempt has been made to preserve the actual language used by American soldiers in World War II. For the convenience of the reader all difficult military and foreign terms are explained in footnotes.

CHAPTER I

In the Philippines

During the day that the March of Death started out of Bataan after the surrender on April 9, 1942, with men dropping from exhaustion or being beaten and killed, I made a simple — or great and terrible — decision. I resolved to survive. To live.[1]

I was a boy just past twenty. My world has changed so much that it does not seem indecent to tell the truth about how I was drafted. My home was in Texas, but I had registered with the Selective Service board at Grants, New Mexico. I had been employed by the Standard Oil Company of California. The rules of that organization were that I obtain a draft registration card. The New Mexico board plucked my number and on March 24, 1941, I was inducted at Fort Bliss, Texas, into the 200th Coast Artillery anti-aircraft regiment, which was to kill, bleed, and sing to the bitter end in the Battle of Bataan. We sailed for the Philippines in September 1941. Instead of making the voyage on a crowded transport, I got the break of boarding a big liner, the *President Coolidge*, with a few other enlisted men, and had luxurious quarters for a buck private.[2]

Upon hearing of the "lucky breaks" that came my way throughout the war and the years of my imprisonment, a friend has spoken insistently of a "protective influence" which worked in my behalf. Be that as it may, it does seem that something always intervened for me in the narrow squeaks over and beyond my resolution to survive.

The Day Before War

Sunday, December 7, 1941, in the Philippine Islands, the day before the stars of war dropped there in astonishing suddenness, was Saturday

7

at home in America. I was stationed at Fort Stotsenburg adjacent to
Clark Flying Field, north of Manila. While my officer-boss sat and
supped in the coolness of a village cantina with his friends, his chauffeur and I, his clerk, waited outside in a command car under the hot
tropical sun. The chauffeur grumbled:

"Few more days of this and I'm going over the hill."

"Yeah, a few more hours and we'll both go," I griped in sympathy.

Just bored soldier rebellion that seldom evolves into absence-with-
out-leave, much less desertion. What I really longed for was a few days
in the gracious city of Manila eighty kilometers away, dressed in civvies*
and free from military duties.

After a time my officer sent out word by a Filipino boy that I could
take the afternoon off. Like most young Yank soldiers in a foreign land
I loved to hike and see things. My curiosity led me to the fringe of the
barrio,† where I watched tiny Pygmies practicing with bows and arrows.
I had dabbled in the study of anthropology. I had been adopted into a
New Mexico Indian tribe. Foreign languages were easy for me. But these
very primitive people soon lost my interest. Besides, it was terrifically
hot under the December sun. I strolled on seeking shade. After a time
I came to a large plantation house. Small Filipino boys were playing
about. With typical Oriental curiosity for anything American, they surrounded me and we talked.

Presently I saw a girl part curtains and walk out on the veranda.
Now, the Filipinos have a soft-spoken, roundabout approach to any delicate subject. Often a third person acts in settling disputes, marriage
arrangements, business affairs. Filipina girls of good breeding possess an
Oriental shyness and reserve. It would be unusual if one spoke first to a
strange man.[3]

This girl was no exception. Though she stepped lightly, her lips
appeared stiff, but it seemed to me that her eyes smiled. I watched as she
seated herself and straightened her white tropical dress. She was a picture of what I imagined Spanish romance to be. I was a twentieth-cen-
tury G.I.; but having lived along the Mexican border in Texas, I knew
how to pluck a guitar and sing a bit. I began to sing a little song I often

*Civilian clothes.
†A country town.

Soldier McBride preparing to leave for war, 1941.

heard along the border, "Adelita." She looked directly at me for the first time. Embarrassed, I stopped. There was a soft-spoken conversation between her and the children. In a moment a small boy bowed politely before me.

"My cousin," he informed me in his slow but good English, "wishes me to tell you that she appreciates you very much."

The charming Eurasian girl was smiling. "Are you the Pearl of the Orient?" I asked her.

She blushed and said, "No, I am Rosalina Flores. My grandfather was an American. You are welcome here in the house of my uncle."

We plunged into boy and girl talk. She had ice-cold mangoes served on a plate. Rosalina showed me the proper way to eat the juicy, dripping fruit with a fork, in case I should ever be with people in the socially high brackets. But I used my fingers and juice dripped from my mouth. We laughed at that, and at nothing. It was great fun, that visit, with no thought or care of what Roosevelt and Kurusu might be talking about in far-off Washington.

Toward dusk my officer, Captain Miller of the USAFFE* Intelligence Department, found me there with Rosalina. As we rode back to our quarters at Fort Stotsenburg over the dark jungle road, we forgot that he was an officer and I an enlisted man. We talked of this and that. I stoked my courage and asked for a pass to Manila, and he said, "Sure, Mac, write it out and I'll sign it in the morning." He asked if I had known Miss Flores long, and chuckled when I said, "Yeah, two hours." I saw Rosalina twice again, long afterward, under circumstances that no human being could have imagined that Sunday afternoon.

Such was my life the day before war began.

News of Pearl Harbor

That night I wrote a three-day pass for Manila and left it on the captain's desk. The next morning I was awakened by an efficient young West Point lieutenant. He was rousing out all the men in my barrack.

"You four, draw guns and ammunition!" he ordered with jabbing

*United States Armed Forces in the Far East.

finger when we were on our feet. "You, place a guard on the radio station. Call the Filipino Scouts. Can anybody fire the reveille gun?"

When nobody volunteered I said I thought I could. I had watched Filipino Scouts fire it and had artillery training. The lieutenant placed three blank shells into my hands.

"Fire three. All three. Hurry. All three, understand! It's the alarm. The Japs have started the war."

I fired one shell. The breech jammed and I could not fire the others. That shot may have been the first in the war on Luzon.

Back in the barrack I heard our radio blaring about an attack at Pearl Harbor. The dumbest G.I. should have known for three days that war was knocking on our doors, because endless truckloads of bombs had been rolling in from Manila, the crews had been at the anti-aircraft guns day and night, all combat men had been ordered to go armed, and our planes had been constantly in the air.

I have been asked what my thoughts were when I found that the war had started. I thought of my unsigned pass on the captain's desk. I went there and tore it savagely into shreds. Goodbye, Manila.

Whether I ate breakfast escapes my memory. Captain Miller had an errand in Tarlac City, forty kilometers away. We drove there. We were back at Fort Stotsenburg by noon. I ate dinner and stepped outside the mess hall. The captain's private car stood where I had left it. I considered driving to the Clark Field Post Exchange (PX) for ice cream to finish off my G.I. dinner. The radio in the lounge room began shouting that Baguio, summer capital of the Philippines far north in Luzon, had been bombed. We learned afterward that the bombing had been light. The large-bodied sergeant standing next to me called out in these exact words[4]:

"Hey, look at our naval air force up there. Boy; that's the Navy!"

The First Bombs Drop

Several of the men, including Sergeant Valencia of Belen, New Mexico, and myself, had been trained at the Fort Bliss anti-aircraft center to identify enemy aircraft. We all yelled together in about the same words: "Our Navy, hell! Those are Jap planes!"

Someone shouted to take cover. Some of the non-combat men crawled under the barracks. Some combat men ran for guns. I got my Browning automatic rifle from under the command car. In a few seconds silvery bombs began to fall from the bellies of the planes. They came screaming. In the space of a prayer — had I thought to say one — explosions were smashing our planes on Clark Field. Debris was flying. I beheld buildings disintegrate with incredible slowness and fall into smoking ruins. The air snapped from concussions. The ground trembled under my feet. Dust began to roll. I and numerous others kept up small-arms fire at the planes. An American major rushed up bawling for me to quit shooting.

"Stop it, dammit, stop it! Those are our planes!"

He seized the barrel of my BAR. A Browning automatic barrel gets almost hot enough under sustained fire to melt. The major flung down the gun with a yelp of surprise and pain. He glanced at his blistered palm. I could clearly see Nipponese insignia on the under wings of the planes. I snatched up my gun and resumed firing — and was not later reprimanded for disobeying orders. We kept shooting as long as the enemy was within reasonable distance. There were 59 bombers in the attack according to my count. Our anti-aircraft cannon shot down five. It was midnight at home in America when the bombing occurred. Three hours later, over Associated Press wires came the terse message FORT STOTSENBURG HAS BEEN ATTACKED. 200 CASUALTIES ARE REPORTED.[5]

After a short breathing spell, fighter planes came down from a high ceiling where they had been lurking to pounce on any of our planes that got in the air. They sprayed their pills all over the field and parade ground. One could hear the bullets thump and ricochet and screech, and could see them kick up puffs of dust like rows of buttons on long coats. It seemed to me that the attack continued half the afternoon. But I accept General Wainwright's published report that it lasted fourteen minutes.[6]

Wrack and Ruin

None of our planes got up. They had no chance. The fliers had come down for dinner and to refuel. The Nips timed their attack to a dot. In the afternoon many of us looked over the shambles. All shops and hangars were destroyed. I counted fifteen of our planes destroyed, some by bombs and some by uncontrollable grass fire. I saw only one untouched. There were six dummy planes on the field. They could not have been distinguished from real planes from the air. They were not hit. The Japanese evidently had exact last-minute information about them. A number of our planes were out of sight, under forest trees away from the runways, and were not damaged. Press releases to American newspapers did not mention the damaged planes.[7]

The Clark Field PX where I had almost gone for ice cream received a direct hit and every man there was killed. Altogether a good many were killed by the raid. Was this the "protective influence" of which my friend had spoken?

That night patrols surrounded the post and field to guard against possible paratroop attack. Several of us were detailed to take instruments and plot the exact position of all lights visible in any direction. I had a B-C* scope. The next day every house and nipa shack where a light had been indicated was investigated for saboteurs and spies.

Also that day some of us were sent out to confiscate every civilian-owned truck suitable for use in hauling troops and supplies. The regular army units were stripped of half their transportation equipment for the native Philippine forces. I found the Filipino civilians cheerfully willing to sacrifice their only means of hauling their newly harvested rice crop. There was one truck with a hundred bags of rice still on it. The owner waved a hand, slapped me on the back and said[8]: "Take it, Joe. Give the rice to your army. Whip those Japs!"

Back to the Flak Guns

In the evening I found Captain Miller with a long face.

"Mac, my boy," he said, "your detached duty job with me is temporarily terminated. You're a trained anti-aircraft gunner. They want you back in your outfit. But I'll have you back here in a few days, soon as this war cools down."

I never got back to him. I returned to Battery D of the 200th. Daily for about two weeks the Nip planes dropped high explosives, incendi-

---

*Battery commander's telescope.

aries and fragmentation bombs. There is a great feeling of power in firing the three-inch flak gun, feeling the shock of the recoil, seeing the black explosive bursts, watching a wing snap off, seeing the craft flame to earth with a terrific wrecking racket. Killing men that way was as impersonal as branding a calf with a hot iron. One thinks only of doing a nice neat job. But with Japs as the game it was more satisfying than shooting ducks.

We G.I.'s began to think the Jap planes would never stop coming. It was pathetic to see one American P-40 fighting it out with eight or more enemy machines, and astonishing how often the lone Yank batted down two or three Nips.

On December 24 our battery commander, Captain Stump of Deming, New Mexico, passed instructions to get the big pneumatic wheels under our guns. It gave us a lift. Something was cooking! That Christmas Eve of 1941 I met some friends from other batteries in an old barn. We shook hands gravely, which was out of character for soldiers.

"Don't know how the hell we're going to get out of this mess," said my staunch friend Sergeant Solly Manassee of Las Cruces, New Mexico "But by the grace of God we'll work it somehow."

"Well, Merry Christmas, you jungle dobies"—such things we said at parting—"and don't forget to hang up your socks to dry."

Movement toward Bataan

Our Christmas gift from General MacArthur was an order to move. Early on Christmas morning we hitched the prime movers to the nine-ton guns and took a ride toward Bataan Peninsula. The retreat—the "planned strategy"—had begun. Two hours of travel and we set up the guns around a road entrance to the peninsula to protect a small auxiliary flying field called Paulino.

When the steel brutes were set, I went on an errand to the nearby barrio of Hermosa. The citizens offered me anything I wished. With time on my hands I chose to visit a lawyer who had a radio. We listened to Christmas music interrupted now and then with snatches of war news. "Hermosa" means beautiful, and it was paradise to me because of the peace and rest. I shall have to live a long time to forget that the Japs unnecessarily destroyed the civilian population of the little village.

When I got back to the battery our Christmas dinner was on boards under a big acacia tree. Men stood around awaiting the signal to pitch in. Already we were getting but two meals a day, and there was always a background of hunger. Suddenly Jap planes appeared. The men at the guns opened fire. Bombs dropped. Some of our men were hit. One died, a day or two later. But hunger doesn't stop at blood. I managed to grab a scrap of beefsteak out of the dinner wreckage, the last fried meat I was to get for over three years.

That evening I saw a Manila newspaper with the banner line MACARTHUR TAKES TO THE FIELD.[9] We got orders at dusk to move. Another jacking up of the steel brutes to roll the heavy tires under. We didn't go far. Another digging to level the guns. Another jacking up to get the wheels on and under. It's no summer zephyr to do all that. It made men sweat and curse. Time and again for a week we moved in and out of places, the names of which I have forgotten. Japs overhead day and night. The eternal thunder of guns and bombs. The war was getting hot — and so was the singing of the 200th. It was famous as "the singing outfit," and we never sang church hymns. Colonel Stephen M. Mellnik described this hectic period in the life of my regiment as follows[10]:

> The successive withdrawals and deployments, to keep pace with the retreating forces, was a nightmare. The skeletonized 200th, covering the retreat of three Infantry Divisions, stretched Napoleon's maxim "Economy of Force" to its elastic limit. No greater Economy of Force could have been made. By judicious use of the 24 hours in each day, and by dispensing with eating and sleeping, the 200th safely convoyed its three divisions into Bataan. "The impossible was accomplished yesterday!"

On the first day of 1942, Battery D, alone, was ordered easterly away from Bataan to cover the important Calumpit Bridge on the road that came up from Manila. It was crucial to hold that bridge so that our forces giving way before the Japanese hordes could get to Bataan, MacArthur's last-stand ground. Our three guns took position near the Manila end of the bridge. The traffic's flow was orderly and unbroken — military supplies, ammunition, American and Filipino soldiers dirty and exhausted, now and then a line of civilians.

Early in the night heavy artillery fire from close by set in. The enemy was riding us hard. Orders came to move across the bridge before it was shot out. We spent the next day fighting off dive bombers. Their spin-

wheels were falling right on top of us. These were four-bladed fan wheels. When they left the planes they were attached to bombs, but they quickly unscrewed themselves. We could never guess where they would hit and grind a gun crew to bloody flesh. We were all jittery. But nobody deserted the guns.

The day before the Japanese hordes entered Manila, long lines of civilian automobiles came over the bridge. They were harried continually by the enemy planes.

Battling Boys of Bataan

Another of our moves started that night. The Japs were hammering close and hard. We rolled through blazing San Fernando, in Pampanga province, with flames so near that our ammunition was in danger. Dive bombers hit a railroad center. From the explosions chunks of oil tank cars whizzed around us. Concussions were continuous. We Yanks were on the run.

Nearing Bataan the next forenoon Battery D sustained its first casualties. Our own noises, the grunt of artillery, covered sounds. Before we knew it planes were right over us dropping their eggs. We flung ourselves to the ground. I got into the shallow rut made by the wheels of a prime mover, on my back. The bombs hit on the other side of the gun. Men were killed. Fragments struck and exploded BAR ammunition magazines on my belt and tore off one of my boots and cut my toes. I clawed frantically to get the sizzling metal and smoldering cloth off my belly. I was burned.

When I saw the remains of my companions I was unnerved. I got off by myself. For an hour, I suppose, I sat numbed, breathing hard, tightening my teeth, my fists, over and over and over. After this fit of nerves was finished, I never thought much about death or being killed as long as I was in combat.

We who were to become the "Battling Bastards of Bataan" had received no unnerving indoctrination regarding the horrors of war before we entered fighting. American boys who followed us into the global war have told me their minds were full of news stories about battle and that their training had been, "You are doing this to keep a Jap or Nazi from killing you," and that they were sensitized to dread before they ever heard a gun crack.

Their emotions were unbalanced by the long training and waiting, by teary letters from home, by goodbyes and last-minute weeping. Men who fought America's first battles experienced no preliminaries. One day we were singing to a beautiful Eurasian girl; the next, we were fighting. There was no time to think of loved ones, or for receiving pats on the back from Uncle Sam and home. About the only attention we got was in the form of congratulatory radio messages received by General MacArthur from such persons as King George, Joseph Stalin, Chiang Kai-shek and Franklin Roosevelt. We remembered the last few words of a message from General Charles de Gaulle to MacArthur and we repeated them sometimes in the thick of fighting. They were simple words, and at that time no one tried to analyze why we used them. I think now it was the message that preceded them which inspired us, and the conclusion was the summing up of something fine. The words were, "Yours today, tomorrow and forever." We considered them a sort of Allied promise that reinforcements would be sent to us.

We Crowd onto Bataan

On the night of January 1, 1942, all American and Philippine troops were moving into the Bataan country, the Japanese pounding us from the air with everything they had, it seemed. The roads were crowded. Progress had to be slow and careful. We were taking up the chosen defense ground of General MacArthur. In time an American line was formed clear cross the peninsula. The objectives of my regiment were airfields down on Manila Bay shore on the east edge of Bataan within sight of Corregidor Island.

The night of January 3 we were still creeping toward those objectives. For the time being the Japs weren't hammering us. There was a bright moon and we could drive without lights. I straddled the barrel of a flak gun as the prime mover tugged us along. Men sang. We struck matches carelessly to smoke the "long brown dobie" cigarettes. We were tired, hungry, just riding along. Hard labor was to start soon.

The objective of Battery D was Bataan Airfield. We had hoped to

arrive early, get the guns set, and sleep till daylight. Our map showed a
road from the highway to the airfield but we found no such road. We
had to chop out thick vegetation, trees, creepers, to the shrilling of startled monkeys and the crawl of huge snakes. Under the canopy of the jungle it was dark. We sometimes had to push the nine-ton guns. When we
got near the field — anti-aircraft weapons are never set up squarely on
the edge of an airfield — we worked more hours removing the wheels.
With the octopus-like outriggers finally spread, it was almost impossible to level the gun platforms. We took turns at swinging sledgeham-
mers to break trenches in the hard rock to make slots for the arms. It
was coming daylight when we at last had the stuff set and camouflaged
with tree branches. But there was one thing we did not know then — we
were set for the duration. We were right there until the surrender.

We Like Battle

The Battle of Bataan began in earnest when Japanese two-motored
bombers began to fly over by the hundreds. They laid their eggs everywhere. Although we realized that this meant destruction for many people we were happy again. Hard and uninteresting labor was ended. We
were back at our guns. That was what we loved, by then. We wanted to
kill, kill, kill. We had become impregnated with battle hate. We sang.

Our observation and warning posts were alert and active: "Heavy
motors in the west! Closer now. At cloud level. Hah, there's the sons of
bitches! Fifty Jap planes. They got the eye on us."

Then the gun commanders: "Power's on. Stand by! On target. Fifty
rounds, rapid fire. Commence — firing!"

We liked to hear those orders. The ammunition handlers — we
should have had ten but had five or six — would lay shells on the platform. The relay man picked them up and put them in the fuse-cutter.
I as fuse-cutter matched my dial with my left hand and with my right
turned the lever that set the time fuse. The relay man lifted the readied
shell to the gun breech. The gunner shoved the shell into the chamber
with his left hand, the breech-block closed automatically, his right hand
jerked the lanyard and fired the gun, and his left foot kicked the ejected
empty hull off the platform. Going well, we could fire thirty shots a

minute. That speed made the gunner look like a dancing man. He was called "the jitterbug."

The Quinine Clipper

We who manned the flak guns behind the so-called front lines wanted to get out for a taste of infantry fighting. Our officers griped and growled that we'd get our bellies full right where we were and said defense of the airfield was more important. The entire Bataan air force consisted of six patched-up P-40 planes and one antique biplane belonging to the Philippine Army. Also there was a slow amphibian salvaged by the Navy which was called the Quinine Clipper because it was used in daring secret night trips to other islands to bring needed quinine to Bataan.

Evidently the Nips were under the delusion that we had a lot of aircraft, because they flew over daily to bomb, and in clear weather they kept a machine circling high over us like a hawk watching a poultry pen.

One day our P-40's went to escort the old biplane on a trip to photograph the Jap gun positions at our old Cavite Navy Yard across Manila Bay. It was piloted by daring Captain Jesus Villamor of the Philippine air corps. The mission was completed and he was returning to Bataan Field when eight Jap Zeros attacked from their hiding places in the high clouds. Our six P-40's leaped up to intercept. This is said to have been the most thrilling dogfight of the war.

On the ground we stood by our guns and watched. We did not dare fire for fear of hitting our own planes. Within a few minutes the Yank pilots had downed three of the enemy. We knew our own planes must soon run out of fuel. We danced and yelled and beat our fists. But with only five planes left to our six the Nips did the usual: turned tail and fled. One P-40 pursued. He cut a Jap motor in two. The plane dropped lower and lower. It came down on the nearby Pilar emergency landing strip between the Jap and American lines. Our field artillery blasted it to small pieces. The next day we heard Jap propagandists on the Manila radio saying, "The barbaric Americans now have a machine which pulls our planes to the ground, where the poor fliers are destroyed." The next day a city newspaper in El Paso, Texas, carried the following brief account of the affair[11]:

> Gen. Douglas MacArthur's tiny American aviation force has taken the air despite overwhelming air superiority, the War Department reported today, shooting down at least four and possibly five enemy planes in a "thrilling encounter" over Bataan Province. A second challenge to the Japanese air force was made by a pair of MacArthur's daredevil motor torpedo boats which tackled a formation of Japanese dive-bombers and disabled at least three.

Starvation Sets In

When my battery retreated to Bataan, we carried about ten days' rations. This was carefully doled out twice a day to the hungry men. Some supplies were sent over from Corregidor. On January 15 I ate my last slice of American-baked bread for more than three years. I was only one among about 70,000 hungry people on Bataan. About half of these were Filipino civilians. When we made our retreat there had been no provision for feeding thousands of noncombatants trapped behind our lines. The high brass became fearful that these people, influenced by Jap propaganda about blood-brotherism and co-prosperity, would turn against us; so we were ordered to share our handfuls of rice with them. There was little evidence that Filipinos ever assisted the Japanese against us.

As the food situation grew worse, our hunger became actual starvation. When we got down to one meal a day it consisted of about a half canteen-cup of dirty, musty boiled rice and six or eight common-size cans of salmon for a hundred men. A buddy, Corporal W. Tixier of Clayton, New Mexico, and I began to make trips into banana groves and such places in the evenings in search of extra food. Thousands of others were doing the same thing. Soon all wild fruit and coconut trees were stripped.

January 24 was my birthday, and the 26th was General MacArthur's. I didn't know how old he was, but I was twenty-something and starving.

By February our men were becoming too weak to serve the guns properly. Some prayed that they would be killed but not before they got one more good hot meal into their stomachs. Corporal Tixier and I made up our minds not to starve. He covered for me one day so that my absence from the gun would not be noted and I went out with my Springfield rifle and all the money and trading articles we could rake together. I contacted an old acquaintance, Federico Chico, a mestizo Chinese and member of the Philippine Constabulary.

Chico had a tongueless boy from the Igorot mountain tribe* of Luzon who assisted the corporal in his work as medical aid man for the constabulary company on beach defense. This boy, named Cruz, possessed a savage's knowledge of jungle trees and plants. Chico took my articles and money and bargained with Filipinos for salt and sent Cruz into the brush with me to begin my education in primitive jungle hunting.

I Became a Hunter

Without a tongue — I never did learn how he lost it — Cruz was unable to make me understand his grunts. He understood only a few English words. But he was uncanny in reading my gestures and thoughts. He showed me a tree which grows the cashew nuts purchasable in the United States in tiny five-cent packages. These nuts are poisonous until properly cleaned and roasted. Cruz showed me that the fruit at the top of the nuts is edible for a starving man. Under his direction I obtained roots and cabbages from other trees and plants. He showed me tree beans that could be boiled into syrup and used for sweetening. A tea was produced by boiling leaves from yet another tree. When we got back to Chico he had salt for me. I was able to return to my buddies with quite a collection of edibles.

Other trips were made. I always returned with something. Most of the boys hesitated to enter the jungle because of the danger of meeting Japs or getting lost. I soon learned to time my trips for when I would not be needed or missed on the gun. The boys began to urge me to do meat-hunting. Unofficially I was detailed for the job. I went out with my rifle nearly every day after that. Everywhere I met Filipino or American soldiers they were quoting a bit of doggerel. Nobody ever knew who composed this masterpiece, but it was on every lip and was something like this:

*A pagan Mongoloid-Indonesian people who have never been completely absorbed into the body politic because of reluctance to abandon head-hunting.

We have no papa and do not care,
    We have no mamma anywhere,
We have no Uncle Sam at all,
    Just the same we'll never fall;
We're the Battling Bastards of Bataan.

We live on rice and carabao,
    We fight and fight only God knows how,
Our tropical fevers always run high,
    And just like rats the Yanks die.
We, the Battling Bastards of Bataan.

If peace comes to this troubled world,
    And we go home to the same old girl,
And if with draft dodger she did wed,
    While we in this stinking jungle bled;
We'll battle the bastard back to Bataan.

Bring your taxes, tariffs and tolls,
    Destroy the weak and disgust the bold.
Communism, socialism, Republicanism too,
    With this sort of living we are through.
    The Battling Bastards of Bataan.

Starvation Stalks Us

We Americans, the first large group of our soldiers ever to be cut off from home supply or quick reinforcements, just couldn't believe that so great a country as ours would desert us. We daily expected a convoy of ships from the States. Each day we looked for this dreamed-of succor. We expected planes, too, because the engineers worked constantly at repairing and enlarging the airports. Surely the three existing airfields and splinter shelters were not just for our six battered P-40's.

Whenever we saw Filipinos shifting rock-loaded barges around the Cabcaben docks the rumors flew that our long-past-due convoy would arrive that night. We knew that if one did come, Japs would make a great effort to prevent a landing, knew there would be plenty of fighting, and knew that some of us would be killed. We were ready to call the bet. We were convoy-happy. No one ever prophesied that it would be three and a half years before those of us who survived would see and touch fresh Yank troops. There was another bit of doggerel recited on Bataan:

When our bones blend with the stones,
You'll hear the parrots cry,
The men who used to own those bones,
Were left by their country to die.

By the time all horses and most of the *carabao*—the water buffalo, the scimitar-horned beast of burden in the Orient—had been killed, there was little meat left. The monkeys, parrots, wild chickens and pigs, even songbirds, had been cleaned from the jungle. Cruz was not always available, but since he had shown me how the natives marked the trails, I could not easily become lost.

The markings were simple. One strip of bark cut from a tree meant that the trail was a Number One. Two or three circles meant second- and third-class paths. Waterhole locations were shown with sticks and stones similar to what Boy Scouts in the States use.

On some of my hunts I took both tongueless Cruz and Lorenzo Pedro Cimmerron, an American Indian boy from Acoma, New Mexico. We hunted wild chickens. These fowls were hard to kill in daytime with a rifle since they ran and flew with extraordinary swiftness in the thick undergrowth. Cimmerron and I learned to wait until late evening to catch these birds after they had gone to roost. We had learned to stalk wild turkeys on Mount Taylor in New Mexico. Creeping up on the jungle dwellers was not much different. We were usually able to shoot two or three point-blank before they exploded off into the shadows.

Returning from one of these twilight hunts we met three Japs on the trail. The situation did not call for argument. We stepped behind mango tree boles and picked off the dim human figures as ruthlessly as we shot chickens. Hunger and safety are seldom squeamish. As we cooked our chickens my Indian friend smiled. He nodded wisely in the way of his people, and said, "Yeah, Mac, we left three chickens back in the brush for the buzzards, but these are for-you-and-me birds."

He was content, waiting for his supper. I was starved, and the first enemy I had ever shot before my eyes did not haunt me either.

A Savage for an Hour

So near starvation were we that I began spending entire days in the manner of Davy Crockett and Daniel Boone. One forenoon Cimmerron and I separated. By midafternoon I had not seen one thing to shoot. I was in an area of Jap signs. But I was famished. I was determined to get food. There was wild game and I meant to find it. Hunger keys a man up, sharpens his sense of sight, of smelling, of hearing to an unbelievable pitch.

I was keyed higher than imagination had ever been. I became conscious of humanly indescribable emotions. With the acute danger of Nips and jungle serpents and other hindrances before me, my mind expanded, strengthened, rather than doing the civilized human thing of taking warning. I no longer felt the restraint of civilized fears. I was a savage. I felt surprising strength in my muscles. My steps lightened. My eyes caught every moving leaf, every trembling shadow. I descended even lower. I became an animal. I melted into the jungle with the sinuous stealth of a panther. I was ready to pounce upon anything that moved.

At that pitch I saw a tiny movement. A raised head. A large jungle cock! He was fifty feet from my rifle. He did not see or hear me. He came on, head bobbing, my way. He was alert but no more alert than I. I raised my rifle with invisible motion, as slow as time. He was flopping on the ground. With an exultant yell I leaped for the threshing feathers and the hot scent of blood.

As I returned to my battery with my kill the tautness gradually flowed out of me. I became drained of emotion. But the memory of that savage interlude, with its sense of degradation, will long remain with me.

I Will Return

On March 21, 1942, General Jonathan Wainwright assumed command of all troops remaining in the Philippines. We received an inspiring message from General MacArthur. His words were similar to the following:

"We have retreated as far as we can retreat. The Japanese have not yet sent as many men against us at one time as we have here. Hundreds of planes and thousands of troops have been dispatched for our relief. Now continue to stand up and fight for your country."

We starving, weary soldiers felt renewed — "hundreds of planes, thousands of troops." Doubtless MacArthur meant they were being sent into the Pacific. But we weren't mind readers. We thought they were near.

The next we heard from the tall general he was in Australia, by the president's orders, and sending back his famous message, "I shall return." When the thousands of Americans on Bataan heard these things we cursed MacArthur, Roosevelt, the Army, the Navy, the American people, and even Charlie McCarthy and ourselves.

Yeah, our griping embraced the world because suddenly we felt so hopeless and starved and cut off—diseased and weary men. Men laughed like devils as they threw phrases about: "Battling Boys of Bataan, ha-ha-ha! MacArthur's Miracle Men—ye gods!" Somebody had said, "We have nothing but praise for the men of Bataan." Nothing but praise was right. "Dammittohell, we want chow, we want ammunition, we want planes. T'hell with praise." But these bitter outbursts only made us more fighting wrathful. We knew we were going to fight it out alone but we'd knock off as many Japs as we could before we died.

Hunter to Fisherman

Along about March it became too hazardous to hunt in the jungle. The Japs were everywhere. Bombs and shells didn't care where they fell. Chico and Cruz introduced me to Filipino fishermen. By helping them I could get a few fish. In a few days I learned a few fishermen's tricks. We took every living thing we caught in the nets and divided it.

Then the fishing boat disappeared. I was haunting the Cabcaben docks for it when far out on Manila Bay I and a few loitering Filipinos saw a small boat with a Nip flag. I was the only one present with a gun. We thought the Japs might be trying to slip in against the American rear. We waited until they came nearer. My rifle was a BAR that day. I fired two clips but dared not use any more ammunition. The shooting brought a scout with a .50-caliber machine gun. He put out in a small motor launch with a crew. He raced and overtook the Nips. He did a finishing-off job. We learned that these Nips were trying to escape after landing at Aguloma Point behind our lines.

In the latter days of Bataan, without the fishing boat, Cruz and I waded along the shore hunting for shallow-water fish, snails, crabs, anything that could be eaten. In imitation of the tongueless Igorot I got to peeling off the shells and eating the insides raw.

Parrot Stew and Jerky

I did make one more hunt in the jungle. I ran across a Filipino who owned a carabao which he wished to butcher, but he couldn't get near the half-wild animal. I shot it for him and he gave me a quarter of the carcass. My gun crew had fresh meat, except what I cut into ribbons, loaded with salt, and dried in the sun. This gave me a supply of jerky that was helpful in hanging onto a little strength.

By chance, when not hunting, I shot a lone green parrot not too unlike a domesticated Polly. I ripped off the pretty feathers and tossed him into a pot. For potatoes I diced green mangoes, and used a jungle seed for pepper. A delicious stew!

Disease and Voice of Freedom

Disease was rampant all over Bataan. Dysentery caught me. There wasn't any use to go to the hospital. They were so jammed that men lay in long lines on stretchers waiting for attention. Members of the gun crew could not help me; some were off in hospitals, some were too weak to do any more than halfway service the gun. I got word to the scout medical aide, Corporal Chico. For several days he walked through the hot jungle to bring me food and medicine. About this time our main hospital, which was plainly marked with a large red cross on its roof, was bombed without mercy. Men, patients, doctors, nurses, were killed. Chico's food and medicine helped me. I got back some strength but, like everyone else, was very thin.

Some of the events of the last days are hazy. Radio-casts and sick men got mixed in my mind, I suppose. We couldn't get newscasts from the States because the Japs had facilities for jamming shortwave stuff. But they couldn't break up our reception of casts from the Islands. Regularly in the evening we would hear "The Star Spangled Banner." Every man would remove his hat, and sometimes a tear would drip. Then would come the announcer's cheery "Good evening, everybody, this is the VOICE OF FREEDOM, speaking from somewhere in the Philippines." An encouraging message from him in the last days of Bataan was that Jap planes had mistakenly dive-bombed and destroyed hundreds of their own men in an air attack over our front lines.

With such lucky breaks as this we clung to hope that something would happen to relieve us.

But what could ground soldiers, made of flesh and blood, do when they were blown from their foxholes by high-explosive bombs and artillery, and were outnumbered fifty to one by fresh enemy troops from Singapore? The Yanks had to withstand that sort of thing and bayonet charges. For days, at the last, there was never a quiet moment on the peninsula. At night the artillery of both sides flashed endlessly; we would hunker and count the seconds until the missiles passed over. From our rear the Nips' metal aimed at Corregidor Island would sometimes pass over and land in our sleeping area. During the last month I never once removed my boots or clothing. At night a man had either to sleep in a tree or be one of the fortunate few to own a hammock. Sleeping on the ground meant savage ants eating at you. In a foxhole a deadly snake might enter and try to coil around a sleeper and squeeze the life out of him, or just coil in cozily to get warm. I did fairly well in trees, having some rope to help me out.

The Retreat Starts Suddenly

As the sun was setting on April 8, those of us left in the gun crew were discussing a tough air raid earlier in the afternoon. We kept hearing loud voices, then the sounds of heavy-motored vehicles. They seemed to be moving along a road a kilometer or so from our position. Somebody said he'd bet a hole in a doughnut the engineers were getting ready for the landing that night or reinforcements from the states.

Half hoping the fellow was right I got permission to go scouting to find out. As I approached the road near Laklakan Point I beheld a jumbled convoy of trucks and gun equipment belonging to the Filipino 88th Field Artillery. A scared sergeant told me, "Las' night, Joe, this outfit retreat. Now we retreat more. Tonight I think everybody retreat." The Nips had smashed our lines.

I watched a few minutes longer. The road began to swarm with infantrymen, Pambusco buses, tractors, walking wounded. Suddenly I realized that it was a flood of desperation.

I made tracks for my outfit. By the time I got to my gun there was general confusion. The crew was darting here and there getting our equipment ready to move.

It was getting dark and Nip bullets were snipping through the brush. Some Filipino artillerymen were firing a huge 155-millimeter gun where they had stopped, right behind us. Its blasts seemed to flatten us. Men cursed and skinned knuckles and hurt arms and knees as we strove frantically to get the big tires under the guns. Finally all the battery's gear was ready. We moved under the shouted orders out over the rough-and-tumble jungle road for the main highway. One prime mover and its gun got stuck on a rock with a high center. We drained the oil from the motor and left it running to burn out. All the tires were split with an axe. We set fire to the ammunition on the mover bed. The resulting explosions momentarily stopped the Nips, who were crowding our heels.

Before we could reach the highway, orders were given to destroy the radar equipment. Men beat it with hammers. Others laid explosives around it. We poured on gasoline and touched a match. The Japs would never learn anything from it!

Ordered to Hold the Japs

The Bataan road was so jammed with vehicles, orders were so confused, that we appeared to move scarcely at all. Finally we parked our equipment off the roadside. Orders came along that the 200th could form a holding line against the Japs at Cabcaben Field. Cabcaben was along the shore about four kilometers farther down the Bataan Field where we had been so long. We became infantrymen on the spot. A non-com handed me and my companion the first grenades we had ever held. I had just time to grab my raincoat and stuff my shirt pockets with my precious jerky. Then we were in a ragged formation heading down the road. It was not until April 1947, that even a brief account of this action was released to the public in an article in the *Coast Artillery Journal*.[12]

> After two days of preparatory fire, the Japs commenced their infantry and tank attacks. The combined Infantry and tank effort broke through our lines. Human beings could just stand so much and no more. The 200th was forced to destroy its antiaircraft equipment and to organize as an infantry unit with the mission of defending the line south of Cabcaben airfield! Disorganized Filipino units were clogging the single road leading to Marivales, while Japanese planes added to the confusion by spraying the road with machine-gun fire. Human beings weakened by hunger and disease, had but one thought — to get away from the slaughter. The 200th stayed anchored to its infantry position south of Cabcaben airfield while the Jap tanks ploughed through the line, interested only in exploiting the break-through. The 200th firmed us forcing the Jap attackers to deploy.

Some of the boys of the 200th began to sing. We saw retreating Filipinos. We hollered for them to help us hold off the Japs. Some started to join us. Our officers ordered them away. We asked for their ammunition. A Filipino hollered back: "Ammo, hell! Joe, we're lucky to escape with a mess kit."

The songs that knots of the 200th sang along the dark, tropical trail were not nice songs. They were reckless and profane and derisive and defiant. At the edge of Cabcaben Field we were ordered to dig foxholes in a line facing the oncoming Japs, and to cut out all singing, talking and smoking so the enemy would not know where we were. Explosions kept shaking the night — our ammunition dumps, we supposed, being blown up behind us. From sickness and bombs we hadn't enough men left for an unbroken line of digging. Our foxholes were about eight feet apart. The line bent around shoreward slightly toward Bataan Field. The Nips attacked on our right flank but were driven back by a few of us men equipped with BARs, by Filipino beach defense units and our remaining P-40. We fired blindly into the darkness wherever we saw the flash from a Nip rifle or mortar. The Nips had landed from small boats in the bay and were trying to bring in 75-millimeter cannon.

At the same time the enemy was cracking our lines on the peninsula's east side, with their reinforcements of troops and planes brought in after the fall of Singapore. As we crouched and waited in our new foxholes a mad jumble of men was piling up around Marivales, six or seven miles to the west.

Earthquake and Grenades

As I finished digging the last foxhole that I was ever to scoop out, there came a shaking of the earth greater than explosions could cause. I sank to my knees. Even Nature was adding her touch to the thunder of the lone big gun firing on Corregidor every five seconds. It was the heaviest earthquake I had been through on Luzon. For a time I was filled with a superstitious fear and dread of I knew not what.

After a time my companion, Lorenzo, whispered from his foxhole for me to sleep two hours while he watched, then he would sleep with me on guard. I slumped down and was asleep. Within an hour a human body was tumbling in on me. Before I could struggle an excited voice was whispering:

"Mac! Mac! The dammed thing's going to bust!"

Thank God not a Nip! Lorenzo. Tinkering with a hand grenade in the darkness he had done something to the release. He'd dropped the thing and sprung for my foxhole. We waited with held breath for the bust and bang that would locate our line for the Nips and bring out our cursing officers. A minute, two minutes, half a lifetime — but the bug didn't burst.

To show Lorenzo what a devil I was I belly-squirmed to his hole, stretched out my arm as long as a pole and felt around. I found the thing. Leaking sweat I flung it into the jungle. It didn't explode. We guessed he hadn't pressed it enough. Suddenly we were rocking with laughter, silly hysterical laughter, until our empty stomachs hurt. Then our idiotic gasping faded away into vacuity and the mad noisy night came back. But we slept no more.

White Rag in Moonlight

The moon heaved up as in a normal world. The landing lights of Cabcaben Field flashed on, right before us. A plane stood there. It took off into the back sky. The lights went out. I did not know it then but Colonel Carlos P. Romulo was aboard that plane. He later was sensationalized in America as "The Last Man out of Bataan." He described the incident in his autobiography in these words[13]:

We pulled the plane out into the clearing. Shells were still falling, but the Japanese had apparently shifted their main fire away from the devastated field and toward the beach. We had to wait for the moon. I sat there listening to the guns and thinking of those poor devils being driven back into the water. I kept looking at my watch. The seconds crawled past. It was eighteen minutes past one, which made it the morning of April ninth, when the moon edged timidly about the blazing jungle.

Half-tracks and tanks noisily shifted position over toward the beach. We listened and waited, and watched for Nips. I wondered if Lorenzo were still there, and the fellow on my other side, in the jungle shadow. They were, for a whisper came along that a jeep full of men had passed off in the moonlight with a white rag held high over their heads, going toward the Japanese.

A rumor stalked in with the dawn that we were surrendering. But it sounded as if battles were still going on — our people exploding the last of the ammunition, no doubt. Nip dive-bombers began to circle. I saw them diving in the distance at some unseen object. Shells began to explode again before my eyes on the landing strip.

Surrender, it seemed, didn't come at the drop of a hat, leaving a clean cut before and after.

Across Cabcaben Field I saw men around the artesian well. I was famished for a drink. Shells were bursting on the field — Corregidor or the Nips, I suppose, trying to prevent its use. I waited until a shell exploded, then ran like a sprinter for water. Clear, cool, gushing water. I stood in it with my shoes. There was no time to wash the dirt off my body and clothing. I drank and drank and filled my canteen. Then as I was running back (between shells, I hoped), an explosion knocked me like a shotgunned rabbit. My legs hurt. They were bleeding. I crawled to my foxhole. I tore off my shirt and wrapped dirty strips around my bleeding lower left leg, without having the courage to explore to see what damage had been done. Years later I was recommended for the Purple Heart medal because of this wound by a kindly officer who remembers the incident. The official paper accompanying the medal read as follows:

GENERAL ORDERS NUMBER 10: Under the provision of Ar 600–45, as amended a Purple Heart is awarded by the Commanding Officer, 29th Replacement Depot, to the following named enlisted man:

Corporal Myrrl W. McBride, 3801228, Coast Artillery Corps, United States Army. For injuries received as a result of enemy action at Bataan, Luzon, Philippine Islands, on 9 April 1942.

Tears and Surrender

Lorenzo, who had been off hunting food, returned empty-handed except for two cigarettes he had scrounged. As we smoked I emptied half my canteen into his. I had just remarked that as soon as the captain came along I would ask to go see the first-aid station about my leg. An order came voice-rattling along the lines:

"Don't fire unless fired upon."

What the hell! How come Yanks couldn't fire on Nips? Before we could adjust to the idea another order came crashing down:

"Do not fire under any circumstances."

We sat slack-jawed, drained out, wondering blankly. Immediately the reason for the order glided down upon Cabcaben Field right before our eyes — a small Jap plane with a single occupant. A smugly grinning, smart-alec-looking Japanese pilot sat in the cockpit. An American captain who I had never seen before stopped nearby. Tears were streaming down his cheeks. I lined my sights on that helmeted head in the cockpit. I didn't shoot. I didn't dare.

But that plane, that tear-washed face, confirmed the surrender rumor. Men crawled in hushed and miserable silence from their holes. The 200th had quit singing. I felt unclean.

Funeral of a Diary

We had received our last American order, about not firing. Our officers said we were on our own. We enlisted men began to set out on our own initiative. I buried what little ammunition I had left, along with the grenades and bolt from my rifle. Weeks before, an order had been circulated for all men to turn in their papers, letters and diaries for storing at Corregidor. Not one in five had responded. I had held on to my diary. Now I reluctantly lifted it from my musette bag. I held it tight in my hands. It was a five-year diary. Texas friends had given it to me for Christmas in 1940. It had a little lock and key. It was all but filled with hoarded names and dates and events. I found a cookie tin and put it inside. I wrapped a burlap sack around the can. I dug a hole under a tree. I marked the tree in my mind, should future occasion ever bring me back. I held the funeral of my diary. I filled the grave. I decorated it with withered leaves and trash to hide the spot.

I did go back years afterward, and what a corpse I found!

First Touch by a Jap

Soon a line of Jap tanks came rumbling along the road toward us, led by an American jeep. Their guns were bearing directly on us as they stopped. An American colonel got out of the jeep and gave us taut-voiced orders to pile our rifles and ammunition. Jap soldiers quickly surrounded us with drawn pistols and fixed bayonets. I shut my eyes and tossed my boltless rifle on the pile growing from the hands of sullen men and moved on, under the gestures and shoving hands of our Jap captors, to a group that was being searched.

Remaining in my bag were a raincoat, a pair of pliers, a spoon, and a canteen cup. The first Jap soldier ever to touch me took the coat and pliers; also my money and watch. He jerked up my old First World War helmet to look inside. That was always a trick of theirs. Then he thumbed me on.

Quite a group of us were marched to the summit of a low hill on the south side of Cabcaben Field, where we found perhaps two hundred Americans and Filipinos, some of them civilians, standing inside a circle of enemy guards. As we joined them we were all pushed around, being made to take intervals from one another as if getting ready for calisthenics. This evidently was so that each person could be observed. Shells were lumbering over us, from a Jap battery on Cabcaben Field firing at the island of Corregidor, and from Corregidor guns returning the fire.

We stood there for perhaps two hours under the now broiling sun. Then a Jap motioned for us to sit. Sitting men had less chance, or restless initiative, to make a break. There were not many guards. Other groups were being gathered everywhere.

The firing over our heads kept up. Thoughtfully, the Corregidor gunners were using armor-piercing shells rather than high explosive. They did some damage to the Jap artillery too. Once they split up a gun and men. But the firing was doing injury to some of our crowd also. I grew desperately afraid that some of the civilians would make a break to get away from the danger. We had been placed on the hill, of course, as a shield for the Japs or a deterrent to the Americans.

The Nip guards were restless too. They were privates without a noncom. They evidently didn't know what to do, were afraid to make a move. Not all the Yanks there were of the 200th. Colonel C. G. Sage of Deming, New Mexico, commander of the regiment, had been scooped in. He must have sensed the hazard of a break, for finally he got carefully to his feet and spoke quietly:

"Everyone move slowly down to the foot of the hill."

He stood there and watched the Jap guards until every person was safely off the hill. I never so admired the action of any man in my life. My colonel!

The guards were as glad as we were to move down. Their acquiescence in the move seems yet to be an apt illustration of what I frequently saw in the ensuing weeks and months and years — the Jap soldier, or officer, often doesn't know what to do and will look to foreigners, even enemies, to direct him.

The Abandoned Canteen

At the bottom of the hill, on the airfield again, the colonel halted us. The guards were not surrounding us too tightly now; some of them had left. A young Filipino girl became panicky and started to run. I grabbed her and got her back with the group. After that my attention wandered to the sea. I saw a British merchantman, the *Yu Sang* it was, apparently at anchor a few hundred yards off toward Corregidor. I moved casually toward the shore with the idea of swimming out to her, resting a while, then swimming on to Corregidor.

I reached the shore and got off my shoes and pants when two Jap cavalrymen came loping down on me with drawn sabers. In a second they had me cut off from the water. I got my legs back into my pants and one foot into a shoe before their threatening sabers forced me to move away, one foot bare. I had no time to snatch up my canteen.

Perhaps it is as well I did not make it. The Britisher was cargoed with all the bombs left in Bataan, with time fuses set, as I learned later. It is history that she blew up right there. That "protective influence" was working in my favor!

The horsemen stopped me where Yank and Filipino prisoners were being jammed on to a truck. I slipped on my other shoe. The two cavalrymen drove me on to a group of about one hundred men, a mixed bunch, most of whom I had never seen. The Japs began moving us along the highway northward.

The March of Death to Camp O'Donnell had begun, though I did not know it. I did not know until years later that it was called the Death March.

CHAPTER II

Death March and Camp O'Donnell

Our Japanese captors marched us along slowly to Bataan Field, where other groups joined our bunch. They looked as starved as me. Many questioned wildly about water. I was thirsty too. I remembered my half-full canteen back on the beach. It was very hot between the jungle walls. Men began to stagger and fall. They were promptly shot or bayoneted.

A Filipino civilian stepped from the roadside into our ranks. A Jap officer promptly shot him in the head with a small pistol. That was an unnecessary, inexcusable crime. Americans around me muttered angrily. One said, "You see that? The bullet didn't go clear through — he won't die for a long time." My friend Master Sergeant John Moseley ordered harshly, "Quit talking about it, you'll get more shot."

Jap Cruelty Begins

We met a long column of Japanese infantry marching in. They had Filipino captives loaded with Jap packs and were leading them by ropes around their necks. Most of the natives were old enough to have wrinkled faces and gray hair. The soldiers were Nip shock troopers. They had been fighting us in the jungle for four months. They felt no kindness for anyone. Bataan was theirs but Corregidor remained in American hands; some of them would be killed in taking it. Their mood was one of mingled dread, resentment and hate.

Japanese trucks, tractors, artillery came moving in. They had better stuff than our 1918 equipment. The line of infantrymen batted us with rifle butts to clear the narrow road. There was no getting completely off; the jungle wall stopped us. We were beaten away, senselessly.

The jaw of a man just ahead of me was crushed by the ram of a rifle butt. Instinctively I slanted my helmet down to protect my own face. For that "impudent and defiant" gesture a Jap seized my arm and deftly dislocated my wrist over his knee. I was to learn that they punished animals with the same childishness. Presently an American medical corpsman reached for my wrist and snapped it back into place.

By the time we had marched eight or ten kilometers I was dragging, sick at my stomach; soaked with sweat in the hot breezeless road, and thirsty. Again I remembered my canteen, gray naked metal without the cover, half full of water, lying there on the sand. Further, I had not eaten for nearly two days. The wound in my leg was throbbing and bleeding again.

Evening darkness came. It was cooler but our lips were swelling for lack of water. The endless line of Jap infantrymen traveling in the opposite direction to us made me dizzy. Finally they stopped. They kindled fires. Apparently every individual made his own fire. They began to cook. We could smell their food. As I saw their greasy, yellow, brutal faces in the flickering lights a strange, hate-inspired thought came to me — cannibals preparing for a human feast.

I tried to forget my miseries by thinking about the Japs. I told myself that they were stupid, blundering, and uncivilized. But that did not give me any of their food. My thinking slowed my steps. I lagged. Suddenly a bayonet jabbed my left shoulder. I felt the point grind on bone. Before I could make up the lagged space I felt another thrust. It was so unnecessary. A touch, a slap on the back, a gesture, would have been sufficient. My head dropped. I wanted to cry. And a wild impulse urged me to throw all my strength at that guard and beat and kill him.

A Decision Is Made

Abruptly I was afraid of my emotions. If I let go and fought back I would be bayoneted or clubbed to death in a brief whirlwind of motions and agony of amazement at leaving the world. Life on This Side was suddenly desirable, something that I desperately wanted to hold on to. And death, in the other pan of the scales, seemed shameful, disgraceful. In a moment, a breath, anger, hate, revenge, sickness all spilled from me as from an upset pail. I would live. I would survive this captivity. I would watch my captors, study their minds, their whimsies, their racial characteristics. I would not be a weakling and an ignoramus and die. I would survive by knowledge. No Jap would ever kill me.

Was this a simple — or a great and terrific — decision? I really do not know. It was a decision to live, and I never faltered from it from that moment. It fortified me in a thousand delicate situations when the caprice of my captors promised death or maiming punishment. It made me bear the unbearable, the filth, the cruelty, the hunger of all those coming prisoner days until I emerged from them alive and free.

Stop for the Night

Eventually the guards halted us. Our heads lifted to the hope for food and water. Now we could eat, drink, rest. Though I had seen all this coast country on my hunting trips I was hazy as to our location. All the road we had covered through the afternoon had been strewn with the corpses of a battlefield — the blackening bodies of dead men giving off that sweetish, sickening smell peculiar to spoiling human flesh; mangled carcasses of horses, machinery, trucks, guns stalled and deserted or blasted out of sane shape; barrios, fishing villages of long-legged nipa* shacks, burned and wrecked beyond recognition.

Where we stopped that night I do not know. Perhaps Limay. We were herded into a carabao pen. A fire had been built in the center of the muddy, filthy enclosure, possibly by captives who were marching ahead of us.

Since returning to the States, I have talked with people who supposed that all captives were marched out of Bataan at the same time, in one long straggling line. They weren't. They were taken out in bunches as the Japs gathered them up. It required something like two weeks to round up all Americans and Filipinos on the peninsula, and they were

---

*Palm leaves used to protect the roof of buildings.

herded along to Camp O'Donnell in large and small contingents. The most I ever heard of being in one group was about a thousand. In my bunch this night there were probably three or four hundred. I do not know; nobody tried to count, I suppose.

In the carabao pen, when we saw the glowing embers in the darkness, we who had cups dipped thick and dirty water smelling of urine from the buffaloes' wallow and set the cups on the coals to boil. As we huddled over them, cursing their slowness, a Jap guard came swinging his rifle and shouting, knocking or backing us away, kicking over our cups into the darkness. We thought he was warning us against the filthy drink. He left, and returned with a five-gallon gasoline can and a pail dripping over with water. Our eyes snapped in grateful eagerness. These Japs weren't so bad after all.

He sloshed the whole pail on the coals, completely extinguishing them.

I managed to find my cup. I did not drink from the wallow. Some did from lack of control and were violently sick. I lay down in a muddy corner of the pen, close against the fence. The enclosure was so jammed that many could not lie down. Mosquitoes and other insects buzzed and bit, and guards tramped just outside the fence, but exhaustion drugged me to sleep.

Death Is Resumed

Very early the next morning we were routed out of the pen, leaving men who had died and men who couldn't rise again.[1] The latter were promptly bayoneted. Without food, without water, we went marching on to we knew not where. By the time we passed the ruins of Orion Town, the day was hot and men were falling out. The Japs resumed their bayonet work. For the record, I myself saw, with my own eyes, at least half a dozen killed before the day was well advanced.

I began using the knowledge I had resolved to use in order to survive. Already I had observed that men at the front of the column fared better than the laggards. I made it a point to get near the head and stay there. With one eye always out for guards, I now studied the Americans tramping along ahead of me, curiously inspecting and analyzing each individual. I wished to understand why and how they kept in the lead. I concluded eventually that it was because they had tough mentalities.

Also I did not fail to observe the surrounding country when the jungle stood aside and permitted. I saw the place where the Japs had their observation balloons. We had often wondered at the battery how they made observations for artillery fire. There were many strange and interesting sights if one thought of such things instead of the miseries. I saw the lead Yanks scanning the countryside too.

We were hurried along at a quick step and covered a good many kilometers that forenoon. A rumor set in that food and water would be given to us at the next stop, and the trucks would carry us on from there. I'll never forget the hope that pumped up in me. At every barrio, or at any buildings, our expectations jumped. But that hope, as hours went on, was not enough for some. They were beyond surviving on the milk of dreams. One old gray-haired American officer who could take it no longer quietly laid himself across the banister of a high bridge, made one more slight effort, and rolled over, to end in a thud far below.

He had cheated the Japs. It gave others ideas. I could tell by the way their eyes rolled and sought for opportunity. But not I. I had survival in my soul. I would live even if my throat cracked — and it almost did. I began to have crazy visions of my naked canteen back on the Cabcaben beach with water in it — water that would slosh. God, if I could stoop and pick it up!

Water, Super-Water!

Finally, in midafternoon, our dragging feet were permitted to stop their leaden, monotonous passing of each other. Because the Jap guards had to be changed. Healthy, watered, fed, they couldn't take what they were making their captives take under the tropical sun. We got water. There were two wells, I remember, and one pipe. We prisoners made a rush. The guards used their clubbed rifles to hold the stampede. They could knock down only a few men. The rest of us reached that pipe like fighting beasts. Only half alive, my throat all but dried shut, unable to bellow at men to quit pushing me, able only to make idiotic sounds, I was in the melee. I couldn't keep out, with the men behind crowding madly.

I got my canteen cup full and managed to break out of the mob. I sat and sipped. Sipped slowly, tasting each drop separately. I had learned in high school football, and in mountain climbing, what gulping water into a hot body would do, but many of the men did not know, or did not care. I had had no water since the previous mid-forenoon on the Cabcaben hill. This water was the clearest, coolest, sweetest, most potent and delicious that ever passed my lips.

Some drank too fast and hurt themselves. Some may not have been able to drink at all. When we moved on we left more dead men on the ground, Americans and Filipinos.

Episode by the Wayside

We marched and marched and marched along the endless blazing road. Then a strange thing happened. I do not know whether it was that day or the next. I must confess that I do not know exactly how many days the Death March lasted. The hours and days and nights became hazy at times. At the time of the queer episode, whether the second or the third day, my mind was gray. That naked canteen of mine, with water in it, came up from the distant beach and moved before me, dancing along, tra-la-la, just beyond my reach. I knew it was real because I could hear the water slosh.

Through the grayness I realized that I was not holding my place toward the head of the column. I tried to speed up, but my steps only became slower. I blacked out completely. I must have fainted while walking. Throbbing of the bayonet spots on my back and the aching of my wounded leg roused me. That and the vague feeling that a Nip guard was close to me. But guard or no guard, I could go no farther. I simply fell down beside the road. The Nip was close. I could see that. I tried to rise before he raised his bayoneted rifle and pinned me to the earth. Then I felt I was past ever rising again.

He gestured for me to get up. I couldn't, but I did raise up on one elbow. My mind was working swiftly all at once. I pointed to my wrist where my watch should have been. I held open my fingers and thumb to indicate five minutes. I made motions that I would go on after a rest.

This man was evidently in charge of the column. Japanese noncommissioned officers have more responsibilities than do American noncoms. A Jap captain is up in the high brass. This noncom must have been tired too, or had some understanding in his Oriental mind. Or quite likely he, with his Japanese sense of inferiority, was ready to listen to a foreigner's judgment. They hate to do things wrong and lay themselves open to American contempt.[2] Whatever the reason, he called commands to other guards. The whole column stopped.

I lay there panting, wondering if he were going to make an example of me before them all. But no, it was rest — life-giving rest. I turned on my back and breathed deeply and regularly. Consciousness and strength renewed in me. Each breath gave me more enjoyment than I ever squeezed out of a whole week before.

We rested probably fifteen minutes. When we moved on I was at the head of the column thinking that, after all, life was worth the price of any circumstance. Maybe such energy and buoyancy came from the realization that I could reason with and influence our captors. The other men were not so lifted. Only the humdrum instincts of their minds carried their feet moving along.

That Jerky Meat

The next day, I suppose it was, there was still no food. Our eyes were sunken. We were dusty ghosts. Men dropped and never got up. My friend Master Sergeant John Moseley began to falter and stumble. He shook his head to let me know he might not go much farther. I tried feebly to encourage him. Just a rusty word or two: "Stay with it."

In the course of the morning — I remembered that it wasn't yet scorching hot — we came to Nip soldiers lined along the road. We were entering an area not touched by battle and destruction. These men seemed at first to be curious onlookers, gawking at bewhiskered, dragging, spiritless American captives. Presently I was noticing that their stares were sharply focused. Then one snatched at the hand of an air corps sergeant. He tried to pull off a finger ring. It would not come off readily. The Jap drew his bayonet, held the finger straight, and whacked it off.

I slipped off my own ring and dropped it furtively into the dust. I felt my pockets for anything the looting Nips might want. I touched my shirt pockets, and felt that jerky meat I had cached there the night before surrender. I had completely forgotten about it! It gave me a terrific boost! When no guard was near I would pinch off an inch or two of a strip in my pocket, duck my head and slip it in my mouth. It smelled and tasted sweaty. Too, it was briny from the curing salt, and I feared would increase my thirst. But the salt seemed to draw moisture into my mouth. Presently I could swallow pretty well over my dry, swollen tongue.

In the midst of this sneak banquet I remembered John Moseley. He was stumbling along. Of course my instinct was to keep all that jerky for myself, to survive. The reaction to that, after some fighting of conscience, was, "I'll be damned if I survive by hurting other people, except the damn Japs." So I worked into my palm a string of the jerky about as long as a hair ribbon. I reached down and touched my knuckles to the back of John's hand. He responded and I slipped the meat into his fist. I saw him look down at his slightly opened fingers. Then his glance shot up to my face. He could not make sounds, but I read the movement of his throat, "God, thanks, Mac!"

Girl Drops a Mango

Along toward noon that day we entered the highway leading to Guagua in the province of Pampanga. Filipino civilians lined the road. They tried to give us fruit and food. The Jap guards resented the attention to us. They tried to keep the natives back. But Filipinos would cry out to attract our notice, dart between bayonets, and get food into the prisoners' hands. Others would toss things over the Nips' heads. I caught a lump of thrown sugar. We began to march under great trees. A Filipino girl up in one of these dropped a mango into my hands. I gave half to John and skated the rest of the oyster-slick juiciness over my tongue and down the hatch. What a delicious fruit is the mango!

We passed through villages of people in clean clothing, children playing and stopping to stare at our bearded faces; heard the musical tinkle and clang of calesa bells, smelled the perfume of sugar refineries. It seemed to me a great big wide and beautiful world after the months of Bataan jungle and hills. It was the land of milk and honey in another language. Lord, how I desired to lie down and stay there.

Sugar Cane Stampede

There was a rest while the guards were changed again. How we envied men who could rest and eat and sit! And how we hated those Japs who wouldn't take what they were ladling out to us. As I lay on the hot ground a smiling Japanese officer squatted beside me and said in broken English for me not to worry, that I would reach my destination safely. I don't know why he did it. It helped me through. That "protective influence" was benefiting me again — if there really was such a force.

Our new guards were a little more considerate. I thought they were quartermaster troops not hardened to combat. They did beat us some with rifles and, as if driving cattle, shouted "*Koora*!" This is a word of many meanings, one being equivalent to our urgent "Hey!" No one was bayoneted for a while.

While the sugar cane seemed to revive some of us, it was death to others. Men with all their strength spent through malaria, dysentery, tropical sun and starvation began to drop by the pairs. The rumor was started that after a rest in the next town we would walk to Manila. We knew Manila was over sixty kilometers away and none of us believed we could walk over a few more miles without food, water and rest. Only those who have suffered a combination of the miseries we endured can understand the varied tortures we lived with. Men who were ill and had thus far survived on the march were more than heroes. Somehow I had been so conditioned that I could not cry like some of the boys, but I felt a grief and pain worse than tears when I saw the shrunken form of a friend whom once I had seen as a free, strong, brown-skinned American Indian boy as we ran up the cool mountain slopes of New Mexico childishly searching for pinon nuts. He suffered from dysentery; it was evident by the odor from his clothes. His eyes were shrunken from fatigue and malaria. I knew he was going to fall soon. The situation was completely foreign and incomprehensible to him. When he fell to the ground I slowed my steps but could not attempt to pick him up, for I felt like falling myself as slowly I placed one foot before the other. The boy recognized me as I passed, and while his eyes flickered he formed my name on his lips. There was a little animal-like whimper and he gritted his teeth with a jerk as a Jap bayonet pierced him through the back of the neck. I looked back and he was still. I both pitied and envied. Another hurt was added to my miseries.

San Fernando, Pampanga

Some time or other after the cane patch we staggered into San Fernando. This is the capital of Pampanga province. It was the burning town that we passed through that night on the retreat to Bataan. There was plenty of water. I drank and drank, and washed, and rested. There was a chow line where white, freshly boiled balls of rice were handed out. They were about the size of pool balls, one to a man. Rice is a flavorless, pasty substance to a normal appetite, but this was my first warm food since the day I had tossed the pretty Polly into the pot. That rice had a taste and savor that I have never been able to detect in any other food.

No breakfast was served but we had water to irrigate our souls. With stiff joints and muscles I sat down by the gate and rested. Three Jap pilots entered. They had English-Japanese dictionaries. One of the officers squatted by me. He seemed harmless and friendly and began to talk. By using his dictionary we were able to get a few ideas across to each other. I asked if he knew where we were being taken. He said Manila. I asked if we must walk. He drew a locomotive in the dust and said "toot-toot." He taught me how to count to twenty in Japanese and I readily remembered up to thirteen. That was no credit to me, as I have an aptitude for tongues. He was unable to pronounce correctly the English words he tried to use.

A Puzzled Question

The Japanese were burning with curiosity about us, and also for military information. A captain gestured several of us together and began to question us in English.

"Why did you people quit fighting? Why did you surrender? Why did you not do as the honorable and brave Japanese soldier does, fight to the death?"

He scanned our unshaven faces. He got shrugs and headshakes. His finger pointed the question at me.

"Well, hell," I said, "I'm young, I don't want to die yet. Why do your soldiers commit suicide?"

He stared at me, vastly puzzled. I realized that he was as full of wonder about Americans as we were about Japanese who fought blindly and foolishly to their death. He didn't grasp our psychology any more than we did theirs.

We Have a Train Ride

About mid-forenoon we were marched to the San Fernando railway station and loaded into boxcars. The tiny Philippine cars were of thin metal and were hot enough inside to brown biscuits, especially after a hundred men were jammed into each box. We were packed too tight to move. Sick men moaned and fainted even before the wheels turned. Men grumbled that they would rather walk than ride in such furnaces. Myself, I felt that whatever our destination, we would at least arrive sooner than on foot.

As soon as the train left the town I knew we were not headed toward Manila. We were going in a northerly direction. We swayed over the narrow-gauge track for several hours in the closed cars, the hundred men leaning back and forth as a single solid mass to the movements of the train. When the door was opened we were at Capas Station, several miles south of Tarlac. We were unloaded and found ourselves in the dry central plain of Luzon, a treeless land. Eight men had died during the train ride. Filipina Red Cross workers were prepared to give us food. They were driven back with bayonets. They gave us news — they said that a group of prisoners ahead of us had been permitted to accept the food. So there were prisoners ahead of us. Where?

Camp O'Donnell

The answer to our burning question came after eight or ten kilometers more of the dreary Death March. We were at the infamous Camp

O'Donnell. It was an old Philippine army training camp. It sat out on that stark, baking plain like trash on a table. Most of it was unfenced. Twenty-seven thousand Filipinos and Americans were to die there within the next six weeks. We had no inkling of that as we marched through a gate and were halted.

We found one small group of mixed prisoners already present. A Captain Stzuniyoshi, a fiery little Jap exhibitionist, made us a speech. He strutted and he shouted and told us through an interpreter words similar to this:

"You are our enemies forever. We hate, we hate you. You are at our mercy now and must obey. The Imperial Japanese forces will drive every American out of the East. Our Greater East-Asia Co-Prosperity plan will succeed. You have mistreated and brutalized the Filipinos. We have fed them. It may be that we shall fight you again and again. This war may last for one hundred years. But now you must salute the Japanese soldiers and bow."

I grow angry yet when I think of that man. From that hour we spoke of ourselves as prisoners and not as soldiers; but we never forgot that we were Americans — neither did the Japs.

The red-dot Japanese flag was flying from poles all over the place. That flaunting rag antagonized us even as we made a wild scramble for water at the single faucet the camp afforded. Fights ensued. I got enough water for myself and a man, Private Frank Morris of New York City, who was too weak to help himself. With moisture in our systems we were introduced to a great stack of burlap filled with old tin cans, salvage from the battlefields that the Japs had provided as cups and food containers. A sardine tin was dealt to me.

General King

Upon our arrival we found that General Edward P. King Jr. was already present as the prisoner-commander of Camp O'Donnell. He had been the senior officer on Bataan after the departure of General MacArthur and the transfer of General Wainwright to the command of Corregidor. He operated, of course, under the direction of the strutting little monkey, Captain Stzuniyoshi — Stinkyso, as the prisoners began to call him.

We were assigned to barracks and busied ourselves getting settled. Other prisoner contingents followed up and kept coming at all hours of the day and night. Men able to get about took it upon themselves to help the helpless. I looked after Frank Morris, helped him to get on his shelf in our barrack. He was dying of malaria and dysentery.

"Mac," he would whisper, "can't you do something? Can't you help me?"

I went to the structure designated as the prison hospital. It was little more than a shed. There I found long rows of diseased and wounded and starving men lying on the ground waiting for doctors. The few Americans and Filipinos with medical knowledge were already so overworked that they could not get around even to supply the men with water and rice. I, who could walk and didn't have malaria, was ashamed to ask for dressing for my wounded leg. I reported back to Frank.

"But Mac, can't you, can't you do something?"

"I'll do something," I told him, and it was a promise.

But the promise could not be readily fulfilled. About all I could do was to keep him in water and do the chow-line shuffle for rice. He would scarcely touch the rice.

General King Watches from Window

As soon as the Japs began to get a semblance of organization out of the immediate first confusion, they separated the Filipinos and Americans, not wanting conspiracies. I started the practice of strolling as near the Filipino section as the guards would permit in hopes of seeing some friend who might get out and go to the Flores hacienda near Fort Stotsenburg and ask Rosalina for drugs and food.

One day a man accosted me whom I did not immediately recognize, he was so thinned down. He was Cruz, the tongueless Igorot. He let me know that my old Chinese compadre, Corporal Chico, was in the camp, sick. He carried notes between the scout and me. Chico pointed out that both Americans and Filipinos were slipping out of the camp on errands of mercy. Why not I? Before I could act I was detailed to a job as messenger for General King.

I suppose I got the detail because of my relatively robust condition;

I could still walk around. A major from the 31st U.S. Infantry was detailed with me. Whenever the general had to make a reply to some Japanese demand, or he demanded more food for the men, or better sanitation, blankets, medicines, or more than that one water hydrant — water conditions were unbelievably bad at first — he would dispatch the major and Private McBride to Stinkyso's headquarters. We had to carry a little Nipponese red-dot flag high over our heads. We had to wait outside and bow to every passing Nip until the interpreter deigned to notice us. The answers we received and carried back to the general were usually in about these words:

"We are very sorry that you are suffering so much. The Imperial Japanese Army did not intend for you to be without food and water and blankets and medicine. There are no more food and water and blankets and medicines than you are getting."

With such supplies not increasing and yet more and more prisoners coming in, I often saw General King standing at his office window watching with furrowed, worried face. I know that he felt a deep concern for his men whom he had been forced to surrender on Bataan. It was a terrific responsibility, there in prison. Years later I was to read that the general reported of our treatment to a Senate judiciary subcommittee. The newspaper report read[3]:

> The man who surrendered American forces on Bataan today urged Congress to provide benefits for soldiers who were beaten and starved as prisoners of the Japanese. Retired Maj. Gen. Edward P. King, Jr., of St. Simon Island, Ga., told a Senate committee many such soldiers were discharged without disability benefits. He predicts they will develop defects in the future. "Medical evidence will say that even though those men show no disability at the present time they will develop defects in the future," he testified. He said the Japanese policy of starving prisoners while working them long hours weakened the hearts of these men. Many have unexpectedly died of heart failure, he added. The stocky general told the committee the starving was deliberate and not because of necessity. "Food was allowed to rot and was thrown away rather than give it to us," he said. King said the Japanese failed completely to live up to their pledge to abide by terms of worldwide agreements on treatment of prisoners of war.

Japs Take a Census

In running about as messenger, I saw a lot about how the camp was being managed. I learned much, too, about the Japanese, their minds, their way of thinking, something of their language. It was knowledge by which I was to survive.

I saw that they were having trouble taking their census of the prisoners. They would get a bunch isolated and counted, and before they could get away there would be a dead one or two. Or the countees would slip from one group to another. Neither the Filipinos nor the Americans were very cooperative with the Greater Co-Prosperity Sphere. Too, the newcomers arriving every few hours would rush for the water faucet if the guards weren't brutally active, and get all tangled up with the crowd already there. Others, too sick to stand and be counted, would melt away from under Jap eyes and lie in the narrow shade of the buildings. When the Japs found them they would not know if they had been counted or not.

I think that of all the men in the camp I felt sorriest for the new arrivals, thirsty and sick and trembling, looking wonderingly at us who had water and rest. I often tried to have water in my bottle for them. I was never any hero, but I was young and my emotions were strained to the limit. No greater appreciation have I ever seen than came from the strangers who drained my bottle and murmured a hoarse "Thanks, buddy!"

Mickey Mouse Money Is Hot

The Japs began building an escape-proof fence completely around the big camp. Before it was completed, when they were beginning to get some order, they required us to remain strictly within our *nipa* and *sawale* — woven split bamboo — huts at night. Sentries prowled to enforce the regulations. It made it difficult for men to relieve themselves at night. Having observed the confusion of the Japs about the counting, I took a chance one evening of missing roll call. I wasn't missed. After that I made it a point never to be counted, for no other reason than to be contrary toward the Nips. I slept under the barrack at night. If one escaped he would not be so readily missed.

At this time — the first four or five days at Camp O'Donnell — the prisoners had not been divided into what was later known as the "blood-brother groups." That was a Nip system of listing ten men together and, if one escaped and was not recaptured, of shooting the remaining nine. During my stay in the camp I did not see any men shot, but a friend who I admired, Captain J. Hazelwood of Albuquerque, New Mexico, and seven or eight other officers were taken from the camp and I never heard of them afterward. They had Japanese "Mickey Mouse" money — worthless or "play" money, as we called it — which the Jap guards had given them on the Death March in exchange for American and Filipino currency. Captain Stinkyso may have suspected them of bribery or other imprudence.

Frank Morris, my New York protégé, was not getting any better. He could not eat much, or any, of the canteen-cup full of rice we were getting daily. Many sick men couldn't. Flies were sickeningly bad around the barracks and the mess line. Upon getting my rice issue I often got as far away as possible to avoid the buzzing pests. Frank couldn't do that. He just kept on with his pleas for me to help him.

Chance for Escape

I began to grow weary of camp confinement and sickness and suffering and death. More and more men were dying every day of malaria and dysentery and starvation. Three days of messengering for General King, resting in the shade most of the time, had got the stiffness out of my joints and I felt better. I had not contracted malaria or dysentery. The bayonet jabs in my back were healing without infection. I heard on Bataan that it was best not to remove shell splinters until proper medicines were available, on the theory that the hot metal seared the flesh and kept it sanitary until correctly handled. My leg did not appear to be getting worse. I just kept it wrapped and hoped nature would do the rest. Chico's hints about men leaving camp kept stalking into my consciousness, though I really did not consider escape. I thought more of getting word to Rosalina to send medicine for Frank and others.

On the morning of the eighth day in O'Donnell I was asked by a sergeant looking for "able" men if I would like to go out with a work party getting posts for the camp fence. He did not know I was the general's messenger. I jumped at the chance. No blame attached to outwitting the Nips, or escaping. I joined about fifty other men leaving in a truck.

The posts were out several kilometers to the west where the short-grass plain gave way to the Zambales Mountains. These were the home of the Negrito Pygmies. We had only a few guards. Like soldiers of any nation when away from their officers, they grew careless. They didn't seem to bother much about our strolling off into the woods. I lugged in a post occasionally so they would not grow suspicious, but I scouted most of the time, wondering how on earth I could get word to Rosalina and her uncle.

Nothing turned up during the day. On the following morning, when the working party had already been counted into the truck I decided to go again. I was no nearer to a plan for escape. I mainly wished to get back into the open, the clean air. Maybe I could find a spring or pool of rainwater this time and bathe and soak my feet. I crawled into the truck without being noticed.

Pygmies to the Rescue

Again in the forest I carried posts for two or three hours. I kept going farther among the trees. By chance I got to an open space of cogon* grass near a ravine. I stood staring around. All at once I was startled by eyes peeping at me from a black head. I knew instantly it was a Pygmy.

The Little People are the unconquered creatures of the Philippines. No one knows their number, I suppose. A census has never been managed. The Spaniards learned to leave them alone. They gave instant loyalty to the American forces in the original occupation of the islands nearly half a century ago. They are said to be the only native people who have been allowed the free run of our army posts. According to most authorities they are the aborigines of the Philippine Islands.[4] Their loyalty to America has never wavered. They hated the Japs.

Glancing over my shoulder and seeing that no guard was watch-

---

*Spanish, Tagalog, Visayan and Bikol word for either of two tall grasses (*Imperata cylindrica koenigii* and *I. exaltata*) of the Philippine Islands.

ing, I crashed the cogon grass and rolled into the ravine. I made it look like the fall of a malaria-sick soldier, in case a guard was looking. A short way off three Pygmies stood under a mango tree. From going on hikes with these little four-foot men before the war, I knew some of their customs. One does not approach them with outstretched hands and say, "Hi, I'm glad to see ya!" They would not have understood my words and manner. However, they have an uncanny ability to almost read a person's mind and understand the major situations of the life of a white soldier. Squatting, I waited for them to make the first move. They had bows and arrows and blow-guns, and I knew they would have poisoned arrows. They bird-chattered among themselves, then came forward, surrounding me, waiting for my move.

I tried to tell them with snatches of English and Spanish and gestures that I desired for them to take a message to the Flores hacienda. It was impossible to get comprehension of this into their little heads. They gave up too and began tugging at my arm and making motions to follow. I thought, "To hell with Camp O'Donnell and the Japs, I'm going to take a chance at this." We started out, except for one Pygmy who remained behind as a lookout.

We went through grass and jungles and over hills for what I guessed was five kilometers. They parted the undergrowth for me as courteously as they had done when I was on pleasure hikes and had tobacco to pay them. I wondered if they knew where they were going, what they were doing, and what I would pay them with. Then we were at their village.

For the first time I saw the almost-doll-houses made of thatch in which they lived. Old women were arriving with bundles of wood on their backs. Still older people and children were sitting under trees. They all came forward in a slow curiosity-eyed welcome. Most of the old women had large goiters under their chins. The village was shabby and dirty and the people only half dressed. All this was in contrast to the background of tall trees and a beautiful jungle opening.

An old woman whom I had seen before near Fort Stotsenburg came forward with a little English and Spanish. Food was offered. I asked for rice. I dreaded to eat the tainted meat or other queer foods which was the diet of these jungle folk. I smiled inwardly — I of the tribe American that strode the earth, begging a handful of rice from the most primitive people of Luzon. From that day on I lost pride about food and where and how I got it.

The old woman asked me why I did not go to the *ricos** for food. She named as rich people three or four families whom I did not know and the Floreses, Rosalina's people. How could the people of the jungle have rice, the peppery, sharp-tongued little lady asked me with asperity. I was given a raw sweet potato.

It required a long time to make it clear that I would go to the Flores home if I knew the way. The old lady comprehended at last and found two young tribesmen to be my guides, on condition that I would pay them with a tin of sardines when we got there. Oddly enough, these people liked fish, but living in the mountains away from the sea, they had never learned to take them.

Rosalina Plays Surgeon

We waited until the Zambales Mountains were casting long concealing shadows before we started. The two little guides knew without being told that we must travel under cover to avoid Japs and strange Filipinos. We kept to the grass and brush. About two and a half hours were required to arrive at the Flores home. It was night but there were lights on in the two-story house. I could hear voices. Beneath an open lighted window I called softly, "Rosalina, Rosalina." They recognized my voice and she and her small cousins came running out.

Rosalina, with the heart and emotions of a young girl, cried a little at sight of my ragged and dirty condition, which was underscored by a nearly full, and ragged, set of whiskers. I had had no opportunity to shave since a long time before the surrender. I looked like a marooned pirate.

Rosalina and her uncle told me that it would be dangerous to remain at their hacienda. With all her native Oriental, practical cleverness and caution Rosalina took charge, her uncle agreeing. She gathered clothing and other things and with the delighted boys set out with me to a farmhouse on the estate, two or three kilometers back against the mountain range. The house was built of poles and small logs, had two rooms, was

*Rich hacienda owners.

clean, well furnished, comfortable, and unoccupied for the reason that the farmer had disappeared and other help could not be obtained. It had been used occasionally as a hideout for Filipinos in disfavor with the Japs. Half a dozen paths fanned away from it into the rough mountains. It was an ideal get-away location.

The following day, with warm food, clean clothing, a shave and bath, I was made over. The second day Rosalina, who had picked up some medical knowledge and first aid learning in her training at the University of the Philippines at Manila, prepared to remove the shrapnel from my leg. She persuaded me to down a few gulps of *tuba*, a mild native beer-like drink.* Then she gently pushed my face away so I couldn't look, and with her slim, careful fingers pulled out two heavy slivers of metal from the wound. My forehead flowed with sweat, but the pain was soon gone.

Six days of rest at the farmhouse and I was back in strength and weight. I let myself think lazily of Camp O'Donnell and Frank Morris and others who needed medicine.

It must be said, though, that it was not the incentive to get medicine that sent me back. It was the grapevine news of Doolittle's raid on Tokyo. It reached us on April 29, 1942, if I remember the date correctly. Rosalina and the kids and I danced circles and laughed and gabbled. It made us suppose the Americans would be back in the Islands right soon.

Return to Prison

Reclothed in my dirty rags, with medicines, sugar and some small cans of food secreted on my person, I struck out for O'Donnell. There were no guides now. The Pygmies had left without their sardines, as the Flores household had none. Under cover I reached the woods where the posts had been. No work party was on the job. I hid my plunder and climbed a high tree. The foliage hid me but permitted me to watch over the bleak landscape. I saw no way of reentering O'Donnell except with a work party.

*A wine made by fermenting the juice of a coconut while it remains in the shell.

It was difficult to analyze my motives at that time. It seemed foolish to return to one of the worst concentration camps of modern times. I was, as Texans say, between a rock and a hard place. The next day no work party had appeared by noon. I was ready to give up without knowing just what I wanted to do or where I wanted to go. I wanted the approval of my group for escaping and being able to bring back news and medicine. I wanted my own body to be free from the diseases prevalent in the concentration camp. Then I saw a truck coming over the treeless plain. It was simple to pick up a post and seep in among the other Americans. I perspired with fear that the guards would notice my freshened condition and the lumps under my clothing. They didn't and there were no Americans who knew me to reveal my secret.

And in my mind was the news of the Doolittle raid.

No Hero

Inside O'Donnell again, that night I sought out Frank Morris, Corporal Tixier, Sergeant Walter Lee, Private Cimmerrone, Sergeant Solly Manassee and others.

"And others" were men of the 200th. Looking back, this seems out of character for me. Before the war I hadn't been too happy with my outfit. I felt at times that I wasn't treated right. No promotion, not even to private first class, came my way. The National Guard element of the regiment said frankly that the old hands were entitled to the gravy. Besides, I was a drafted man. Further, I was a Texan and not a citizen of New Mexico. Moreover, I had inadvertently given mortal offense to an officer of the regiment in asking him — tactlessly, but in a friendly way — if I had seen him driving a taxi in a red light district of Albuquerque. And I say now in all sincerity that on Bataan and now in O'Donnell, I could not hold resentment against these sick and weary, nerve-shocked men. I do not today. They were punished more severely than I would ever have wished them to have been.

That night I passed out the medicine and the insignificant quantity of food along with the news of the Doolittle raid. The story didn't take. The men were not skeptical, they were just plain indifferent; they didn't give a damn. There were too many false rumors. These men had been disillusioned too many times before; they were hopeless and hungry. I felt as if I had been slapped. Nor was I any sort of a hero for returning with the medicines. Other men had gone out and returned with more drugs and food than I brought. Whose bright-haired lad did I think I was? Well, I was still a boy; I have learned since then.

CHAPTER III

Contact with Guerrillas

The morning following my return to Camp O'Donnell an American sergeant asked me if I would like to go out on a work detail. I was sick of the stink of dysentery and death. A vision of the cool, clean forest rose before me. I did not refuse. The party was being made up. I joined the usual group of fifty at a truck. I supposed we were going out for more posts, but we moved in a different direction, northerly toward Lingayan Bay.

Our first stop was at a small town named San Fabian. We were herded into a Filipino movie theater. Here we remained two days. The Japs supplied us with sufficient rice, vegetables and fruit to fill our stomachs. Friendly Filipinos managed to toss us tobacco, sugar and bananas. There was plenty of water and we bathed, washed clothing, relaxed. The Japs kept strict guard but did not object to our getting the food from the natives. Clever monkeys! They were fattening us for the kill by hard labor.

From San Fabian we moved out in smaller groups but together. The trucks went on northward over a paved highway that was so near to the long, smooth Lingayen shore that the high tide sometimes splashed on the road. It was cool and pleasant May weather. There were no beatings, no dying men; the breeze was fresh and we were all in good spirits.

As we kept on northward there were fewer signs of Japanese occupation. The Filipinos were smiling and happy. We stopped for the night at a seacoast village called Tagudin, and I began to wonder if it were the Nips who had conquered Luzon or the crafty Filipinos were absorbing the Imperial Japanese "strutting roosters." The Japs were distinctly in the Number Two position, without realizing it.

There was something mocking in the atmosphere. A mischievousness among the young. Straight hard looks at us prisoners from grown men and women, with a twinkle of amusement now and then. Filipino children would do a Maypole circle around a Jap officer and gaily sing, "Who's Afraid of the Big Bad Wolf?" I may not have mentioned that most Filipino youngsters in the towns spoke English with little or no Spanish. It has been said that it took 100,000 American soldiers to gain military control of the Philippines in the 1898 campaign, but one thousand American schoolteachers more thoroughly conquered the population and healed the antagonisms of the people who had been shot at only a few months before.[1] At any rate, the Japanese did not understand much English and thought they were being loved and honored by the sweet kiddies. Or if they did catch the meaning of the words, they probably supposed the big bad wolf idea was a compliment to brave conquerors. The Japanese mind functions in such a pattern that the majority of Nip soldiers thought that every part of the reaction of the Filipinos toward them was all a part of a plan which had been directed from Tokyo.[2]

These kiddies knew plenty of American songs. They sang "God Bless America" for us prisoners. It sort of gripped the throat. The Filipinos just about consider that song the national anthem of the United States.

Something Cooking

I caught a distinct impression in Tagudin that there was something cooking against the Japs. Further, we prisoners had surprising freedom. My group was directed to sleep on the ground under a long-legged nipa shack, with only two guards on duty. A few Americans at a time were permitted to cross the street to a Filipino residence to use the latrine. We managed a little covert talk with Filipinos. Several of them were loitering in the yard and many more in the street. I learned here that the Doolittle raid had been exaggerated into a story that Tokyo was being bombed daily by the Yanks.

Now and then, in the crowd of curious onlookers filling the street, I saw a young healthy Filipino male of army age. His clothes might be ragged and hillbilly, yet he might be wearing American G.I. shoes or have the air and straightness that gave away his being a soldier. Small detachments of the Filipino Army had been cut off in the mountains and had not been able to retreat to Bataan. These had hidden in the mountains and jungle and had not as yet surrendered. Some of these men furtively gave me the "V for Victory" sign with a gesture and a cigarette between V'd fingers, or with hand down against pants leg. When no guard was looking some would make eyes and motions which I interpreted to mean that men were in the adjacent hills with guns.

Yes, something was cooking and it wasn't rice.

Tipoff to Guerrilla Leader

Filipinos in the yard were slipping tuba wine to our men. None of the Americans were paying any attention to what the natives were trying to tell us. So often men were like that, thinking more of bellies than business. Usually they were the ones who took the beatings or got sick and died. My immediate group of nine or ten prisoners were mostly from the 803rd Engineers and were strangers to me. I remember the names of two, Captain Elgin Radcliffe of Pennsylvania and Sergeant Sotnikoff. They took an interest in the drama around us.

When it came my chance to return to the latrine I eagerly opened talk with the Filipino men standing about. Two gave me sharp attention. They told me to return in an hour. When I guessed that the proper time had passed I returned without the guards noticing. They also had been drinking tuba. Back at the sleeping place a few minutes later I had a scrap of paper clutched in my sweating palm. When the guard nearest me dozed, I unfolded the paper in the dim light of the breeze-swaying lantern. It was an unsigned typewritten message in English:

"Major Cushing has already learned of your imprisonment and whereabouts. He will liberate you when the time comes. Do not be afraid, because he knows where you are. There is no war news right now because the radios are being taken up by the Japanese. Keep your chin up."

I was to hear many tales of the daring guerrilla leader Major Cushing, but was never to meet him. However, I saw his work and some of his men, so I have faith in at least some of the legends enthusiastic Filipinos built up around him. To them he was a hero and a bold man. He hated the Japs and he hated Filipino traitors quite as much.

The note may have been written by the major himself for all I knew. It was disappointing because it was not an invitation to join him. In effect it said, "Stay where you are for the time being." Perhaps he knew that if some of us got away there would be suffering for the remaining Americans and some of the Filipinos. He might have had a variety of good reasons.

Camouflaged As Japs

As our convoy moved on northward the next morning, I asked our Nipponese interpreter where we were going. He curled his lip and said slangily, "Don't worry." Despite his uppishness I nagged a few Jap words out of him. Out of my resolve to survive I was improving my vocabulary.

We traveled on through Narvacan and Bengued until we reached a river. The Japs spent the remainder of the day ferrying the convoy across the bridgeless stream. We were in Abra province now. The mountains became higher, the physical appearance of the natives changed, and we rolled through areas of uninhabited country. We were in Igorot territory.

We were issued ragged Japanese army clothing with helmets. There was a cunning back of this. The country was soon to have plenty of snipers. They wished to confuse the unseen riflemen and save their own hides at the cost of ours as much as possible. With our tanned skins and new outfits we had the looks of Japs, even fairly close up, but I declined to accept the change and was not compelled to do so. I wore an Illocano straw hat, shorts and my now ragged G.I. shoes.

We stopped over one night at a town named Laganingalang. It had a nice high school building but it seemed to be the last outpost of civilization. Despite the non-invitation of Cushing's note, I thought more and more about escape as we kept on into the wilderness. Every time I glanced at a Jap-camouflaged American I thought of snipers. I took to keeping my canteen — I had another one now — well filled. Also I secreted a can of salmon in the truck along with a tiny bag of rice. My eyes searched constantly every pile of Nip equipment for an axe. I had concluded that the best way to escape from a guard was to use an axe.

So obsessed was I with the idea that I failed to be practical and figure out what I would do if I didn't get an axe. I paid for my lack of an open mind.

The Headless Guard

Axes, like all tools in the Jap army, were scarce. By evening of the day I decided on an axe as the fatal weapon, I had failed to acquire one. With my closed mind I didn't have the makings of any other plan. I was sent off the trail some distance to a pool of water with several of our captors to wash mess pots and pans. One Nip remained when the others returned. Now was my chance to strike and take it on the lam, as prison stories say. But no axe. Just empty hands and head. The opportunity frayed out.

We had two guards over us that night but one slept. Still I had no plan without an axe. I did not speak to any of the other prisoners about escape. They were constantly quarreling among themselves. I felt that people who quarreled over childish things, such as who did the most work, or got the most to eat, or what Eastern ball team would win the pennant, did not have escape qualities. They wouldn't act quickly in a pinch or be dependable. Yeah, I who couldn't think of anything but an axe, felt that way about them.

In the morning as we prepared to leave, the Jap private with whom I remained at the pool was missing and could nowhere be found. At last his body, minus his head, was discovered near the pool. What if the Nips had seen me toying with an axe! "Protective influence" again? For some reason the Japs accepted my word that he had been alive when he sent me back to camp. Maybe I had an honest face!

Igorots Join Us

With that headless body in mind my escape ardor cooled. The killing suggested bolos.* Bolos suggested head-hunters. The wild country belonged to the Igorots and their brothers-in-culture, the Ifugaos. I

---

*A long knife with a wide blade which is used for cutting away jungle undergrowth and in farming.

had heard little stories about these people's indulging yet in their ancestral sport of drying heads to decorate their tribal halls. Filipino scouts and mining men from the region had told me, however, that the tribal halls had never held a white man's head. That wasn't much reassurance. With war on, there was no telling what might be the mood or whim of the first native one met in the jungle.

No doubt I was overcautious. For as we started out that morning short our trucks — they had gone as far as they could on the narrowing trail and had been sent back — a herd of about fifteen Indian cattle with their Igorot drivers had been added to the party as beasts of burden. We prisoners marched with them. Jap infantrymen were in the land and cavalry and horse-drawn artillery followed. We had become quite an expedition. Each Yank carried heavy loads of equipment.

I stoked up friendliness with an Igorot who could handle English. He said he and his pals had been forced into this job. When no guard was near he hung the weighty steel parts I was carrying over the back of his cow. We doubled our fists, winked at each other, and sealed a mutual understanding of our opinions of the Japs. Nice guy, that head-hunter.

We entered the country of those amazing rice field terraces on mountain slopes, pictures of which I had seen and marveled over in American magazines years before. We were right in the middle of marvelous handmade scenery.

Igorot Thrashes Nip

A little sniping from the terraces set in. It prodded the Nips to hurry. Once they ignored sundown and kept on into the night. We had to travel the narrow ledge-trail in single file. I don't know how the field guns got past. The night was dark except that every fourth man carried a lighted candle. At an exceptionally narrow spot a sleepy Jap soldier stumbled and pitched over the brink. He thumped and thudded and screamed, clear to the bottom. The column did not stop. I kept trudging along under a heavy load, unmoved by the loss of some mother's son, not caring a continental how many more went over. When I became aware of my callousness I was startled. I must have been growing hard.

Another incident left me exultant. It happened on another night, in the damp and cold springtime of the mountains. A little group of us had a fire on the ground and were huddled in its smoke trying to absorb warmth when a Japanese stalked up with a shovel to get some coals. He scooped up most of the fire. The temper of a little Igorot flared. He seized the shovel and shook the embers off. The Jap private slapped him. The Igorot jerked the shovel from his hands and slapped back, sent the private staggering. A Jap sergeant heard or saw the commotion and came running, fumbling out his pistol to shoot. The Igorot swung the shovel and slapped the sergeant down. He whacked again. Then he flung the shovel down and became only a fleeing shadow in the jungle, no doubt ripe to dry a Japanese head for the tribal hall. I hoped to meet him again and give him a ten-dollar bill I had snugged away in my rags.

Men with the Hoes

The sniping increased. Usually it was a Nip who stopped the lead. The shots were coming from the rice terraces. Hundreds of the tribesmen were trained soldiers. They had managed to get guns. The Japs complained bitterly after a sniping that when they got to the rice field workers they would find only a hoe instead of a rifle. "The man with the hoe" became a joke to us prisoners who knew of the famous poem by Markham.

Sometimes we met parties of independent-looking Igorots on the trail. I would try to talk with them but usually received only smiles. They didn't understand. Now and then, however, one with a hoe over his shoulder, in token of his innocence, would speak out, "Hi, Joe, how's it? You okay?" They told me they had learned English in the army or, with pride, at the University of Manila.

If the Japs had their troubles, so did I: beri-beri. It's a malnutrition disease of the tropics. It starts in the extremities and works up into the limbs. I was beginning to feel a premonitory, unpleasant tingling in my toes and fingers.

Survival Knowledge

One day we came to where thoughtful guerrillas had dynamited a trail. A bridge had to be hung against the slope before we could go on.

We prisoners and natives had to carry heavy logs that Japs were felling. At first we worked two men to the log. The Japs tried to make us run. We couldn't. We didn't have the strength; so they put one man to the log. The Igorots showed with scowling faces how little they liked the job. They got themselves bowled over now and then by rifle-butts.

An Igorot and I were returning to the log pile when a smart Jap cavalry lieutenant appeared, bent on speeding up the work. There was one huge log in front of the pile which each slave had ignored for lighter burdens. The officer ordered my little Igorot companion to carry it. The Igorot scowled and backed off. Mr. Nip pulled his pistol. It was obviously impossible for the small native to lift the timber. I stooped to help him. The officer brushed me back. He kicked the Igorot and pointed at the log. The native began to jabber angrily. In a flare of rage the lieutenant shot him through the head. Then, with the man kicking on the ground, the officer motioned for me to take up the timber. I knew that I couldn't lift it. So right then I put into play some of my acquired knowledge of the Japanese.

Scared and angry at the brutal murder, I still managed to smile. A big, blooming, beaming smile. I motioned for him to put his pistol up. I pointed to his strong arms and my thin ones. He indicated for me to pick up the log or he would shoot. I bent and with prodigious effort managed to lift one end. I nodded for him to take the other end. He began to raise his pistol, but I persisted. I got one knee under the log end and held up two fingers, the customary sign of the Japanese for two men to act. I continued my beaming smile. Slowly he reholstered the gun, struck me on the head with his fist, and got to the other end of the timber.

I think the explanation of this lies between my smile and the fact that the Japs don't like to be observed by Americans in poor judgment. It was poor judgment for him to expect one man to carry the log, and he knew it.

We strained and hunched the weight to our shoulders. We staggered along. Before we reached the bridge site he became winded and signed to drop the burden. When he got his breath he came back and slapped my cheeks. This, to "save face." He ordered two passing Igorots to carry the log. With them looking on he slapped me once again. Jap officers slap their men too; it is a customary punishment. Then he smiled at me and led the way to a stump, where we sat and rested. After that I always got a slap and a smile whenever I met this peculiar individual.

There was one bright spot in these days. Wild strawberries. They grow abundantly in these mountains. They were of ordinary size and as tasty as the fruit at home. We picked and ate them at every opportunity along the trail.

I Fake Malaria

After a week or so of the hard trail work I was losing strength. I saw our captors permit two Americans to lie down to rest because they were ill with malaria. This was one disease the Japs feared. When we complained of other sickness, we were beaten, or shorted on food, or put to carrying heavier loads. On impulse I told our interpreter that I too had malaria. He cursed me in two languages for a malingerer and I felt guilty but did not refuse when he told me to lie down with the other two.

The rest ended in our having to go on, without loads, but in the afternoon a Pambusco bus — seats and top but no sides — caught up with the column, carrying supplies. When it was unloaded, it started back with us three as passengers bound for a hospital. Soon the driver and guard were discussing us with grim laughter. It had the ugly sound of an intention to shoot us and reporting that we had attempted to escape. At least we thought that. Then they fell silent and took to watching the roadside as if looking for a likely spot that would never be marked X. About then the motor coughed and stopped. "This is it," said one of the men.

The Japs got out and began to tinker with the engine. The mechanically untrained, heavy-in-the-head farm boys had no idea, apparently, what to do about it. Taking a chance, I got out and offered to help. They stood aside hopefully. It was nothing but a coughing carburetor. In a few minutes the motor was chugging along. So relieved were the two that they gave me friendly smiles and cigarettes — and no more calculating looks. No doubt they were depending on me, after that, to get them to their destination and save them from catching Hail Columbia from their officers.

En route that night we stayed in an old Filipino house of sturdy logs while clouds and rain swept the mountain slopes. The next day we arrived back at the town with the long name, Laganingalang, where a field hospital was in operation in the agricultural high school. My two malarial companions and I were given a room to ourselves, isolated, with a mosquito net and a single blanket each. I soon was feeling rested. Twice a day food and water were sent in for us in a pail, as if for pet coons. A Jap doctor gave us small doses of quinine daily. Malaria was one thing they did their best to cure.

The Grumbler Emerges

About the third day I sat and watched one of my companions die. There was little I could do for him. The Nips told me to bury him in the school grounds. Passing Filipinos helped me dig the grave. It was shallow. A Jap medical corpsman helped drop the body into it. The dead man had no dog tag, nor anything to cover him except his ragged and dirty garments. I shoveled on the dirt. No prayer of commitment. No nothing. He was just another victim of the war. I had seen too many to shed even one tear.

The grave-digging made me weary. Next day I just lay around and rested in our room. It had been the museum and experimental laboratory of the agricultural school. The stuffed animals with their glassy eyes, the dark walls, did not brighten my mood. My remaining companion was a man whom I had nicknamed the Grumbler. He was very ill and had a temper to go with it.

"I'll be damned if I'll eat this stinking Jap chow," he complained to me. He was eternally complaining, and he expected to be waited on as if I were a hired flunky. I tried to persuade him to take the quinine. He was an American soldier, and whether I liked him or not I meant to do my best to help him. I was to meet him again farther on.

Barber with a Gun

To escape the Grumbler's complaining and whining I moved to the porch and sat against the wall in the pleasant sun. Passing Filipinos, seeing my lean, unshaven face and long ragged hair, would look away from the sight. Without my being aware of how he got there, a Filipino man was all at once standing before me. He had a bag hung around his neck and a stool in his hands, which he unfolded. He was a typical street barber. He proceeded to give me a shave and haircut. Busy Nip orderlies passed us but apparently supposed he had been ordered to neaten me up and gave us no attention. In an interval when no Nips passed he suddenly lifted his shirt and displayed an automatic pistol against his brown skin. He spoke low and rapidly:

"Don't worry, Joe. Everything will be okay. We know Major Cushing. He was here a few days ago before the Nips arrived, getting recruits. Now listen, if there is any trouble tomorrow night you stay inside and keep low. Savvy? What's your name?"

I told him my name but he must have forgotten promptly for in an hour a small boy came with a slip of paper for me to write it. I had little confidence in the barber's talk.

That same day a Jap medical captain came in and gave me and the Grumbler a thorough going over. He told me I did not have malaria and could not be hospitalized more than a week longer. His name was Masatoku — will ever I forget it! — and he spoke excellent English. He asked where I was from and when I said Texas, he beamed.

"Oh, I was in Dallas," he said, "attending their state centennial in 1936. Do you know Mr. Blank in Dallas?"

I soon caught that this slant-eyed, smooth-tongued gent had traveled all over my home country before the war. My insides began to yell "Spy!" He quickly sensed my abhorrence and stopped talking in the middle of a sentence to inform me that I would soon be sent back to the mountains for work. He ordered the Grumbler to be removed at once. Months later, in Baguio, Captain Masatoku was responsible for my first public torture.

The Barber Was Right

I was lonesome without the Grumbler despite his complaining. I lay on the porch wishing Filipinos would drop in with some fruit, or to talk. But none came. I realized all at once that the town seemed empty.

That night I pulled down my mosquito net early. In the dark and silent room among the staring specimens, I thought of home and school and all the boys with whom I had played football, and I wondered if by now they were in the army or navy. In the midst of my near self-pity there came a sudden blast of firing all around the school structure.

That good old phrase, "pandemonium" reigned, describes what took place. Bullets broke window glass and splintered doors and thumped against the walls. I guessed that Garand rifles and Browning automatic rifles were being used. The firing sounded like a whole infantry company on Bataan. My first impulse was to rush out and join the guerrillas. I remembered that old absurdity: Bullets ain't got no eyes to see who they hit. So common sense kept me inside. I did peep into the hall when the shooting slackened off a bit. The Japs were running around in confusion. Two were being treated for wounds. From outside came a pained yell; another one had been hit.

At last all the Nips were inside the building, apparently. The firing stopped. I moved my sleeping mat into a long specimen closet so as not to be seen if some Nip peeped into the big room. At dawn motors roared. I looked out. The Nips were loading supplies. With daylight they pulled out. They had forgotten me. I did not feel slighted.

I remained in my room, just in case Jap lurkers might have been left behind. I was weak and hungry, but as hours passed no Filipinos showed up. I wouldn't take a chance in daylight — I wanted to get away when darkness came. Late in the afternoon footsteps sounded in the school building. I got into the specimen closet to watch. After a time Filipino boys entered the room. They searched desks and shelves. I stepped out. The three kids looked as guilty as if caught by teacher. They explained that they had instructions to search for anything the Japs might have left. Who instructed them? They shook their heads, their young mouths tightening. Could they get me in touch with Major Cushing or some guerrilla leader? More head shakes, but they did offer to show me a hut where I would be safe if the Nips returned.

I was so hungry and weak that I could hardly walk. Outside I saw only very old or very young Filipinos. No one could or would give me information as to where the able-bodied population had gone. An old crone gave me some food. I had about one hundred sixty pesos that the people at Tagudin had given me. I bought some supplies and went to the hut. In the morning I struck out for a barrio several kilometers back along the road we had come here on. It was the nearest place I knew of. I had been unable to buy a pistol in Laganingalang, but an old man had given me a bolo on condition that I would cut off Nip heads with it.

Girls Will Be Girls

As I approached the barrio hours later, I hid for a while, watching. Finally three Igorot girls with crude farming implements came along. I stepped out, smiling, giving them the rush with all the Tagalog, Igorot, Illocano, Spanish and English words that I could toss out on the spur of the moment. They didn't understand a word, but they giggled and smiled.

I made signs that I wanted food, water and a gun. I thought they got the idea. They started back toward the barrio. I did not follow. They looked back at me, and smiled and waited. They pointed toward the town. As I had seen no Japs during my watch I hastened to join the maidens. They broke into a run. I decided they were afraid and stopped. They stopped. Waited. When I go up to them they ran again. Then I understood. They wanted to race. The three primitive damsels had very short legs but they gave me a run for my money. When I was winded, they passed me with squeals of laughter. War hadn't dulled their capacity for amusement. In the village they gave the other gals, and old folks, to understand that I was their bargain and they took me to a nipa shack and began cooking a pot of nice fresh rice.

After eating I proceeded to business. I drew pictures on a banana leaf with a fingernail, trying to make them understand that I wished to join guerrillas. By this time several older men and women had gathered at the foot of the ladder up to the long-legged shack. One of the girls sat in the door and used her foot to keep them out, but an old man ran the gauntlet of legs and stood before me smiling. A nice gray old fellow who gave me the V sign and immediately left.

If these people really knew the meaning of V for Victory, I thought, Major Cushing or some guerrilla lieutenant might be in the offing. I thanked the girls with nods and smiles and got outside. Another old man looked at my bolo, shook his head, and proceeded to sharpen it with a stone. Presently the first old man returned and gave me a note in pencil on a paper sack:

"Travel to the East and declare your nationality at every house. You will be taken care of."

Forbidding Country

Having some confidence in these mysterious messages, I was half persuaded to respond to this one. I studied maps of Luzon which I had found in the Laganingalang school. They showed a big hunk of country to the east marked "unexplored." Another chart said that the area was the stomping grounds of the reputedly head-hunting Ifugaos and Bontocs. It was now the middle of May 1942. On the sixth, Corregidor had fallen, which at that time I did not know. Neither did I know that all large bands of guerrillas were being shifted and split into small groups, some surrendering in obedience to General Wainwright's orders.

While I spent three days in the primitive barrio hoping for another message and trying to find out how I could join free fighting forces, I did not know that there was great confusion among the guerrilla elements. Both Americans and Filipinos were torn between the desire to obey the surrender order and to continue hiding, fighting and killing the enemy.

A sudden upsurge of Jap traffic on the nearby road was the dynamite that made me decide to hunt safer territory.

My decision was to respond to the last note and head for the unexplored country, "declaring my nationality at every house." Still having plenty of pesos, I hired guides, got supplies, and set out. A day's travel failed to reveal a single house. Nor did we meet a human being. It was the emptiest and most forbidding land I had seen. Rough and rugged, too, and difficult for me to travel over. I began to suspect that note. Who had written it?

I considered where I could go if I did not go on. Apparently there was no use to go back to the emptied-out town of Laganingalang. Narvacan, through which I had passed coming north with the Japs, seemed to be the nearest town where civilization and organization against the invaders might be found. So I said to the Igorot guides, "Narvacan."

They guided me carefully along back trails away from where Nips might be encountered. We walked slowly, for I was not yet strong but was gaining slowly on three good meals a day. My mind was relaxed; I was enjoying the jungle. The Igorots kept in communication with their people by beating on bamboo drums to send word ahead of us. What they could put over with their bush telegraph was amazing. We would lay low when the hollow, far-traveling booms came back to us that Nips were near. At mealtimes we would always find someone at the trailside with rice and vegetables. Now and then a human figure would emerge from shadows with information. I tried to regulate a balanced diet in hopes the beri-beri tingling would recede, but I learned that it takes more than a few days to straighten out malnutrition difficulties. The starvation of Bataan was but five weeks behind me.

Four-Leaf Clover Luck

Nearing Narvacan we found a deserted nipa house at the edge of the hills. Two kilometers or so distant, across a valley, we could see the town along the seashore. The guides were paid off and I settled down to my own cooking for two days. Clay pots were on hand for utensils. Then I had to get supplies. I made myself known to children at the edge of the town and they assisted with guerrilla grins.

Within a day adults learned about the American soldier hiding out alone. They sent meals up to me. Soon in my prowling I met a young Filipino who had attended a reserve officers' training camp, and I bought a Springfield army rifle from him. A kindly, middle-aged Filipino woman, Mrs. Maria Genoi, came to see me. She said her husband had been a major in the Philippine army and had died at Camp O'Donnell. She and her friends took steady interest in my welfare. They made the hut comfortable. Filipinos were forever concerned about us Yanks; they were saddened when we were in distress. Neat young girls who had studied domestic science in American-managed high schools brought what they considered typical American dishes, such as fish cooked in too much grease, and sea crabs. It was all very nice.

The first rains passed and the sun shone again. I was happy and my mind was functioning in ordinary channels. Sometimes there were noises in the valley. They made me alert for Nips. I always carried my rifle in the crook of my elbow. Before long I learned that the talking and rattling of vehicles came from the natives. So I would grow lax and leave my rifle against a tree. I enjoyed this escape in the pleasant forest. It was stimulating to be able to enjoy the birds, the tropical plants, the various kinds of trees and forget about war and Japs, for a few days at least. A patch of clover grew near my hut. I spent hours looking for four-leaf clover. I had never had time to look for one before in my life, and I did not find one then, but four-leaf clover luck held anyhow.

Lazy "Vacation" Days

In the afternoons boys and girls came up from Narvacan with made-in-America games, such as Monopoly. My visitors never tired of hearing about my home country. To them America was the magic land of the world. When I expressed a desire to get in touch with active guerrillas they advised me against it. Aren't you getting along all right here? Why make trouble for yourself? With vacation laziness I fell in with their ideas. I was enjoying life and recovering my health. The only ink in the water was that sometimes my ankles were swollen from beriberi. Without news of the war I made boasts to my friends that American troops would be fighting again within six months on Philippine soil.

Eventually curiosity got the best of me and I went down into Narvacan to visit. Nip trucks often passed through but no troops had yet made a search of the village or stopped except for brief layovers. It would be easy, I thought, to skip back to my hideout. I spent long evenings there dancing with three charming Illocano* schoolteachers, talking to the local politicians, and describing the Battle of Bataan. Knowledge of my presence was kept from unreliable people — made unreliable by their fear of Japanese retaliation should I be discovered.

Finally this rest period was broken when I was called upon to participate in activities which I am not as yet at liberty to speak of in detail.

---

*The people inhabiting the northern seacoast of Luzon. They are tall, light-complected, Christian, and possess classic facial features.

The following excerpts of a letter from the War Department explains, in part, the situation[3]:

> Personnel who have evaded, escaped, or have been released from Liberated Areas may relate stories of their experiences after clearance with WDBPR, but no reference may be made to:
>
> (1) Existence of unannounced organizations established to assist evaders, escapers or to methods employed by the organization.
>
> (2) Treacherous actions of Allied Prisoners of War or evaders.
>
> (3) Sabotage activities of Allied Prisoners of War whether escaped or detained.
>
> By order of the Secretary of War

I was away from Narvacan for a week and when I returned I was physically exhausted and needed more rest. I resumed my loafing by the hour. Eventually I was going to the shore of evenings for a cool swim. With my naked torso, shorts, and Illocano straw hat, I passed easily for a native in the shadows. I became acquainted with fishermen who invited me to go along in their outrigger canoes. Their fishing was done at night and they were careful to keep their takes out of sight of greedy Jap eyes. The Japs love to eat fish. We placed candles in floating glass balls and the fish, attracted by the light, were easily scooped up in nets.

Coral Can Be Sharp

Moonlight fishing along the jungle-fringed Luzon coast was a delightful experience. It also gave me the personal satisfaction that I was useful to the society which was feeding and caring for me. But the beautiful waters had their knives. One night we were sailing in for a landing some kilometers from our usual place of making shore; for a message had reported that a few Nips were in town. A small son of Mrs. Genoi, who was my constant companion and interpreter, and I decided to go over the side and swim in. The water was smooth and warm and we were reaching shallow depths when I felt my hand strike something sharp.

I stopped swimming and stood. Instantly my feet were cut. I stepped about to escape the sharp things. With each step my feet were cut more. The moon-bright water darkened with my blood. I tried crawling and my hands were lanced anew.

When I at last staggered up on to the beach, young Genoi was there ahead of me, his hands and feet bleeding too. The fishermen carried him home; and although I tried to walk they were soon carrying me also. An ROTC cadet who had some first-aid knowledge dressed my injuries. After three days my hands and legs became infected and began to swell over and above the beri-beri swelling.

After two days Mrs. Genoi's little boy had died. It was very sad. I was somewhat frightened and helpless. Friends urged that I be moved to the home of Dr. Molan. He was the only physician within a hundred-mile area. I consented to be moved to his home. The busy doctor was able to give me attention between his urgent calls, but my hands and legs seemed to grow worse. In Narvacan, as in every village of the whole world, I suppose, there were factions. Many observers have said that an apparent weakness in the old Philippine Commonwealth was the failure of minority groups to throw aside their rivalries and differences to merge into a unified political body.[4] People opposed to the clan of Dr. Molan, Mrs. Genoi and other citizens actively loyal to the United States got wind of my presence in the physician's home. One morning I awakened to find several persons in my room. One was a Jap private with a rifle and another was a Japanese artillery officer who examined my feet to see if I was able to walk.

Again a Prisoner

The officer decided that I could not walk. They carried me by stretcher to a truck in a convoy that was soon heading southward along the coastal highway. Near Candon the convoy was fired upon by people in the hills. There was the usual Japanese confusion and surprise. I raised up to see the fun. We detoured. Back on the road we came to a wooden bridge that was on fire — another detour — another burning bridge. It was detour after detour, for every bridge we came to had been either burned or dynamited. Also, the road had been mined in one place and the truck ahead of mine with its human cargo was blown to smithereens. More "protective influence" for me? I remembered that a group of serious Filipinos had asked me if it would be a good idea to get explosives from mines in the hills and blow up bridges. I had told them it looked like a mighty good idea. Now they, I supposed, were at it with a vengeance.

Despite the obstacles we reached San Fernando that day. Not the San Fernando of Pampanga province near Bataan, but San Fernando in La Union province. I did not feel too badly about being a prisoner; I had escaped before, I could do it again. I was counting my fish too soon.

At San Fernando I was again placed in a high school building which was the Nip hospital. The Japs always picked on stone buildings; they stopped bullets better than nipa walls.

There were eight other hospitalized Americans. There were no other Yanks in the town. I found my old sidekick the Grumbler among them, complaining as consistently as ever. After two weeks I was recovering. I still couldn't put my feet into my leather shoes but could creep about in soft sandals.

The hospital diet of eternal rice and vegetable soup wasn't satisfying to our American stomachs. I ventured from the building into the schoolyard, the Nips making no objection. Soon Filipinos took notice of me. A Miss Carmen Flores, who had been a teacher in the school, contacted me through the fence. She brought tobacco, soap, fruit, sugar and other articles for all of us prisoners. I was the go-between because I was the strongest man.

We had one man named Baynes, from Pennsylvania, who was losing his mind. The Grumbler never gave us any rest. Sergeant Macejewski, who had served in the French Foreign Legion, and I became good friends. He was recovering from malaria. We had endless talks. He possessed an enthusiasm for escaping but wasn't sufficiently recovered to attempt it. We spent much time caring for the others, who were always quarreling among themselves. Macejewski would get deeply disgusted and curse them and try to shut them up. He had little success.

Schooling in Japanese

Doctor Captain Yamamoto was in charge of the hospital. He had plenty of lead-sick Jap patients beside us. He was friendly and took an interest in us Americans as much as in his own people because, he said, the district colonel had ordered him to get us well so that we could go back to work.

From the first Dr. Yamamoto was friendly to me to improve his English so that he could talk to the Filipino girls. He picked me because I was physically able to converse by the hour. He knew book English pretty well but his pronunciation was terrific. I swapped my English for his Japanese, and got the best of the trade. In no time I had quite a stock of sentences.

As I have said, a captain of the Japanese is high brass. So high that a buck private or even a sergeant can become rattled in their presence and not get orders straight. My association with Yamamoto, practically on equal terms, gave me face with the Nip hospital attendants and guards. I often talked the hoi-polloi into taking me to the town streets or along the seashore on the ground that their captain wished me to get plenty of exercise. The captain got on to my tricks, but he desired too much to improve his English to object. Besides, he was a good fellow even if he was a Jap — I'll tell the truth if I'm hanged for it.

When the Cat's Away

Like soldiers the world over, the Japs liked to talk about women. Here in the Islands they had seen uncensored American films for the first time. They couldn't believe their eyes about the association of men and women and the women's independence. They asked a trillion questions and I added to my Japanese by stumblingly answering in their tongue. They had to prompt me with their words to hear about the strange doings of the States. Making more friends all the time, I persuaded two privates on an occasion when Yamamoto was away to take me clear into the town's public market. At the entrance they diffidently waited outside. One reason was that they did not relish knives and dreaded to get into native crowds.

Immediately Filipinos flocked around me. They pressed money into my hands. In San Fernando and later in Baguio, the generous-hearted Filipinos gave me so much money that out of plain shame I refused to take more. Here, they loaded me with bags of fruit and this and that. A woman rushed up to me and said with a kind of peculiar humility, as if she had murdered my brother, "I have a confession to make. My husband was an American." She thrust thirty pesos into my fingers before I knew what she was doing, and flitted away. Her manner was pathetic, somehow, and I have often wondered why she acted in that manner.

When I left the market I was staggering like an overburdened Santa Claus. The guards helped me lug the stuff to the hospital.

Famous Victory Pants

I had arrived at the hospital in shorts that were pretty frayed and ragged. A young San Fernando woman, Miss Josephine N. Salanga, came sometimes to the fence with a package. She must have taken pity on me, for one day she gave me a pair of white duck shorts that she had made. On the back she had sewed a large *V* in colored cloth. We called them my Victory pants, and I promised to wear them in a Victory parade in Manila some day. That V was flaunted before Japanese eyes for several weeks without their knowing what it meant.

Speaking of V's, I chalked up a big one on the stone wall outside under my window. The Japs didn't savvy that either, but the Filipinos did, and how! Once as I stood in the window a native girl of about fourteen came along the street. She was very fat. She did not see me, but she saw the chalked letter. She studied it, and slowly a smile began to dawn. It grew to a grin. I saw her fat body quiver with mirth, and as she went on she tipped back her head and laughed and laughed. She had a joke on the Japs.

The Grumbler Cashes In

Sergeant Macejewski and I looked after the sick constantly, but others took no interest at all in helping, not even in carrying a drink of water to men of their own organization whom they had known for years. The Grumbler was a tough example. He complained and lived while others died, but finally he stopped eating, from contrariness as much as anything, and became too weak to move or talk. Dr. Yamamoto had already given him blood transfusions. Now he gave injections which revived the patient somewhat.

The Grumbler's stomach was in bad condition. Dr. Yamamoto gave me strict orders — I was his assistant now in various capacities — not to let him have any food but soft-boiled rice. The Grumbler kicked like a thrown steer at taking it. I held his nose and fed him anyhow, for his own good. He regained some strength, enough to rise up on an elbow frequently and yell at me for cigarettes or the urinal pail.

I took some ice cream into the ward. Not ice cream à la American. It was goat's milk and crushed mangoes, chilled, for the townspeople had some icing facilities. The Grumbler yelped for some. I refused, backed by the doctor's orders and my own experience that chilled food and dysentery stomachs are not fond brothers. As some of the other men ate the delicacy the Grumbler raised to a sitting posture on his cot and screamed at me, "You dirty whorehouse sons of bitches, you won't even give a dying man some ice cream."

With that he lay back and died.

A Funeral in Style

I wangled permission from Captain Yamamoto to bury the body in the nearby Filipino cemetery. Sergeant Macejewski was down that day. I went alone to dig the grave. Because of so much guerrilla trouble in the country the Japanese district colonel had given strict orders against either his soldiers or the prisoners fraternizing with the Filipinos. So my contact with the natives had to be under cover. The doctor had seen me violate the regulation several times and had looked the other way, knowing I would be discreet when the colonel was around. Now, out of sight of the hospital, a couple of Filipinos came by and offered to help me finish the grave. I did not say no. My part of the digging done, I returned to the hospital for the body.

The Americans who might have been able to give me a hand grunted that they did not feel like it. They were just contrarily agin' helpin' to bury the Grumbler. There was nobody else to help me. I got a rope around his torso and another about his legs and began to pull him the two blocks to the cemetery. Nobody appeared to lend a hand. Sometimes I lugged him like a bale of hay, bumping against my knees. I won't say that I did not drag him part of the way. Even his skeleton body was heavy to me. No one was at the grave when I arrived. I dumped him in and covered him up.

I never was in a good mood when I had to bury people, especially if they had made no effort to survive. I got pretty angry now as I thought of how the Japs could do their deed. I'd seen them light candles at the head and set food by the bodies, even cooked chicken garnished with rice. All I could think of to do was paraphrase some Scripture: "What profiteth a man that he indulge his complaining and lose all his friends?"

That seemed pretty short. Getting angrier, I yanked up an old, weathered, nameless cross from another grave and jammed it into the loose earth of the new one. I penciled on the gray wood the name and date and "803rd Engineers." By this time I had taken the names of all the Americans in the hospital and filed them with the mayor. I went now to him and reported the death of the Grumbler and watched to see that he put it in the cemetery record. Then I found the village priest and asked him to say something. That night by the light of a candle he performed a ritual at the cemetery. It didn't include chicken and dumplings, but there was at least a prayer.

Message from the Jungle

I sent out word that I was interested in escaping. Filipinos brought in replies. But by this time the Pennsylvanian, Bayne, was in critical condition. I was afraid I would have to bury him. Another boy, from my old 200th regiment, Private Pedro Leyva, was suffering from a head wound that had paralyzed him so that he could not walk. With the exception of Sergeant Macejewski every man was too weak to do much for himself. I hated to walk out on them.

One day I received a typewritten letter by grapevine on U.S. Army stationery with the printed heading "In The Field." It was signed, "Captain Barnett, Infantry." I can recall his words pretty accurately:

> I learned of your presence from Mr. Blank. I wonder if you would like to be out here with me? We know how you are living and eating and probably could give you better care here. After about two kilometers from town

you will be comparatively safe. I wonder if it would be worthwhile to make a raid on San Fernando? I have been reading your messages of encouragement that you have been sending out to the people over the country. The followers you have made and many others are ready and willing to help the American Army. We have offered our assistance in hopes we can do something for you. You can get in touch with me through Mr. Blank or other friends. I have four Americans and about four hundred armed men under my command. There are others elsewhere. After reading your message we would like to meet you. Incidentally we aren't guerrillas and will not surrender to anyone.

Encouragement to Filipinos

The message that the letter referred to was this: In my prowling around the school-hospital, I had found equipment in a storeroom. There were typewriters and mimeograph machines. It struck me as a good idea to get out something to counteract the Japs' propaganda. I found history books and read up about Philippine patriots and heroes such as Rizal, whose statue I had seen in Manila. He had come to his end at the hands of the Spaniards long before.

I typed out a long, sentimental, editorial-like "Message to Filipinos" telling them their fathers, husbands and brothers had suffered and died like Rizal on Bataan, on the Death March, and at Camp O'Donnell. I asked them to remember the words of freedom for which Rizal had died. I assured them that the Americans would eventually liberate them from the Japanese masters. I reminded them of MacArthur's words, "I shall return." From hearing some war news I knew that Germany must be taken care of before Japan got hers, so I made it clear that the Philippines still had a long, hard wait ahead. The typing filled two pages. I mimeographed them in considerable quantity and always carried a few in my clothing to pass to Filipinos whom I considered reliable. Since returning to the United States I have received letters from several Filipinos explaining that they still have copies of the message. One of these letters from a Filipino friend reads in part as follows[5]:

> We escaped to the mountain region on September 22, 1944 after the bombing. We brought with us two dresses for each person and secretly carried your letter to us in 1942 and the American flag given us by the American prisoners. When we were in the mountains the Japanese Military Police

wanted us. They had to look from the country, but as soon as they were coming to the mountain where we were, we had already heard the news that they wanted our family by the Filipino underground and we were in our hiding places. It was very risky to carry those two articles across the Japanese line. While in the mountain regions we ate root crops, shells found in rivers and things not poisonous found in forest.

I did not send a decisive reply to Captain Barnett, for a reason I considered good — there was nobody to look after the helpless Yanks. As for myself, the beri-beri persisted but was not too bad.

For a while I stood at my window in the evenings and looked at the purple jungle. I thought of Captain Barnett. He was one of the men General MacArthur had ordered to escape from Bataan and help organize guerrilla units for intelligence work. The captain and others were scattered over the islands doing their best to enlist Filipino assistance in obtaining radio equipment so that information could be sent to the U.S. Headquarters in Australia. Eventually supplies for this purpose were delivered by American submarines.[6]

Cleverness Supplies Food

Without the food furnished us by Filipinos we would have been racked with starvation, for the Nips who served us our rice and soup rations never bothered to see if we had enough. One who helped us was Miss Salanga. She was a daring girl who managed to get a bottle of goat's milk now and then, fresh fish when obtainable, and other foods. Due largely to her efforts we never had to go to bed hungry at night. She had imagination, cunning and courage. Because of the district colonel's orders for "no fraternization" she would have been shot had she been caught in her activities.

Miss Salanga found various ways of smuggling in the supplies. Several times they reached us in the box of a shoeshine boy who was permitted the run of the school. Sometimes I would get them at the fence. Once, when every other method failed, she tied them to a dog and I whistled. The animal knocked me over as he jumped into a window. Soon after my return to the States in September 1945, I received a letter from her which is reproduced here and shows how she operated and how the Filipinos suffered from the war[7]:

Dear Myrrl:

I read in Yank Magazine that most of the American war prisoners have been sent home. I have not heard about you since you went away from San Fernando in 1942. I wrote the War Department in Washington and they tell me your address and that you are still alive. Then yesterday the whole family was extremely happy when we received your letter and learned you are in good health. No tongue can express our happiness for your survival. We cried when we read your letter and learned you are in good health. No tongue can express our happiness for your survival. We cried when we read your letter because it remind us of the many hardships we went through together.

You know four days before you left San Fernando for Baguio, I and my little sister were almost caught by a Japanese soldier in your concentration camp while delivering the "Precious Packages" to the Filipino cooks for delivery to you and the other boys. You called the food precious package although they amount to almost nothing. We got the packages from the cooks and ran with my little sister thru the banana groves and escaped. Back home we changed our dresses with black and rearranged our hairs. Then we returned to your camp and succeeded in giving the packages for delivery to you. It was risky but thrilling. I had no much fear of the Japs. I can't imagine why. God helped us.

When you were in San Fernando we operated in this manner. Father used to go to the country to buy chickens and eggs and mother purchased meat and ingredients. We placed them in a basket and at the top laced fruits. Then sister Adelina and I did the delivery under the pretense of selling fruits to the Japs in your camp. Father hiked 129 kilometers to Baguio and returned to get the quinine and other medicine we gave you the cloth we sewed as your Victory Pants.

The whole La Union Province was placed under martial law from September to December 1942. We could not travel to neighbors places. There was orders to kill all male persons from 14 to 60 years old. It was a terrible period.

In March 1944 we noticed the Japanese were uneasy. We knew of course from the underground radio news that the Yanks were getting closer to the Philippines. In June many Japs landed in San Fernando by swimming; many were wounded and had burned faces. We heard artillery shots far away in the sea. On September 22 San Fernando point was bombed. In December there was heavy shelling from the sea. There was only small houses left standing. The place which was your concentration camp is only slightly damage and your room is not destroyed.

When the bombing started we all went to the country and the Japs looted our food and clothes. Even when we hid our things in the woods, or dug them into the ground the enemy can find them. If we try to get them back they let us face their guns or bayonets. When Uncle Sam and our army came to redeem us the Japs began to massacre all the people. We all ran to the mountains. Everybody in our family is safe but all our aunts and cousins were killed.

Don't think much of the food we used to give you while in prison. We were sorry our money was limited so we could give you only little. We know you were sacrificing for the Philippines so we got to help you. You are our hero for life and our best American witness that we stood with your people in time of darkship and hardship. We didn't go to school this year because we had not enough clothing when the school opened last July.

My family are extending their best regards to you and good luck from me. Write soon.

Read Before Firing

Dr. Yamamoto and an artillery officer took me in their car to see an extensive yardage of supplies and artillery pieces. They asked me to read and explain directions on a small British 75-millimeter cannon which they wished to fire. The gun had apparently been captured at Singapore. The simple words which confused them were, "To unlock turn left." The doctor understood the words but not just what to do. I saw no harm in opening the breech. As they stood closing and opening it, I read another instruction on the recoil cylinder. It said, "Do not fire gun unless oil is at proper level." With my body shutting off their view I unscrewed a tap and let oil drain out far below the level mark. After Captain Yamamoto and I returned to the hospital, I heard artillery fire. That evening the artillery officer was carried in on a stretcher with his chest bleeding. I do not know that the draining of the oil caused the accident.

My Execution

Our Jap sergeant-major at the hospital was a good humored, big-stomached, jolly person who treated me as an equal because I was Captain Yamamoto's language instructor. He too was trying to learn English and had a Japanese-English dictionary. When he wished to talk with me he spoke the simple words in his tongue which I could understand, then would run his finger down the dictionary columns to find other words. His name was Fokunika, which means "long happiness." We had many not unhappy hours together. He was one of the few Nips who took my status as prisoner as a joke and no more than the fortunes of war, holding no grudge because I was an enemy.

One day this chubby, smiling extrovert led me by an arm to his office, gave me an outfit of new clean clothing, and served fruit and ice tea. He and his staff were all smiles and politeness as they jabbered at me. Finally, to put over what they were attempting, Fokunika opened the dictionary and ran down to a word which he underlined with his fingernail, very definitely. The word was *execution*. Observing my statement he laughed and said:

"Yas, yas, you tonight ex-e-cu-shun."

He continued in simple words of his own tongue to explain that many Filipinos would see me, that I must be shaved, bathed and in the fresh clothes he had brought, promptly at seven o'clock. I glanced out the window to see if it might be snowing, I felt so chilly. I thought that at last these smiling Orientals, who had treated me so decently, were through playing cat-and-mouse and were preparing me for death. I remembered the old American custom of giving a condemned man a last good meal before the *execution*. I wondered if they would place a candle and garnished chicken by my side, and decided if they did I would rouse myself long enough to eat it.

As I bowed and started away they reminded me, "Seven o'clock prompt." Before an hour passed, Fokunika came to see that I was bathing and dressing. When I had finished he took me back to his office. I got my eye on a hefty paperweight, meaning to chunk him on his big head, fly through the window like a pigeon, and break down the jungle getting away. Before it seemed the moment to act, Fokunika found another word in the dictionary, *practice*, and handed me a guitar. Then he managed:

"You tonight — execution Filipino danzu moosic."

They only wished me to play for a dance, but they might as well have executed me and saved my nerves. To this day I have recurrent, itchy little suspicions that they may have discovered the meaning of the V's on my pants and under the window and had been paying me back in Japanese coinage.

Move to Baguio

Always in the back of my mind was the idea of joining Captain Barnett. I saw no good reason for his raiding the town and possibly sacrificing the lives of some of his men to liberate a few weak and disabled Americans. To my way of seeing it, his healthy soldiers in the field were of more value than sick men. It was a cold-blooded way to look at it, but prisoners at the mercy of their captors must be fairly practical.

My idea was to get the hospitalized Americans into a condition to sneak out on our own legs. Or we could start a rebellion of our own and make off in the usual confusion that was sure to result. As for my pulling out alone, well, we were hearing tales that the Japs were using their "blood-brother groups," killing all the men of a group if one escaped. I hesitated to cause the death of my patients.

The necessity for a decision was taken out of my hands. Around the middle of July, unexpected orders came for our hospital staff and patients to move to Baguio, about twenty kilometers up into the mountains from San Fernando. Baguio had long been the summer capital of the Philippines. Under the American regime it had been built into as clean and pleasant a city as could be found in the States.[8] The military post, Camp John Hay, was there.

Word of our removal got around swiftly. I received a grapevine tipoff to jump and run for it if we traveled on a road close to the village named Banaue. Our Filipino well-wishers at San Fernando lined the streets to wave goodbye. The Japanese thought the farewell was for them and fairly wiggled with pleasure. I watched for Banaue, but if we got near such a town I did not know it. I just kept rolling along beside three Yanks on their stretchers.

Volunteers for K.P.

The first night at Camp John Hay we were placed in the old Officers' Club with about fifty other sick prisoners. Most of these were men who had been working at a sawmill in the mountains, getting out lumber for the Japs, and had become too weak to continue, due to neglect and insufficient food.

Dr. Yamamoto went with us on the move but he was not in charge at John Hay. That shift lost me my rabbit's foot. There were better nurses than I. I wasn't sick and beri-beri wasn't enough to rate hospital space. So when the Nips asked for volunteer K.P.'s, I took on the kitchen job along with Sergeant Macejewski, of the French Foreign Legion.

Here in the high mountains of North Luzon grew pine trees and other temperate zone plants. Within the camp we had a feeling of being in America. But it did not take long for the Japs to make it look like moving day. They had set up tents and open-air bathing facilities and such like on the charming grounds of the White House and destroyed landscaping that had taken years to create. These lower-bracket Nipponese heathen from the serfdom age just didn't know how to fall in with modern plumbing. So they quit trying to use the bathtubs and showers. They set up large steel gasoline drums in the middle of flower beds, built fires under them, and heated the water.

One barrel would serve fifty to a hundred men, it seemed to me, with reheating. The high brass would climb in naked and wash, then the next grade, and on down in prestige to the sergeants and humble privates. By the time the last Private Nishi got his wetting he looked to be about as muddy as when he went in.

When ready fuel wood gave out the Nips began to break up furniture. Though they liked music, I saw the fine wood of at least eight pianos go to the flames. Electric refrigerators and cooling apparatus were beyond the heathen. They just plain did not understand or trust household machinery, so they would pull out motors and stick cake ice into the spaces of electric refrigerators.

Ammunition for "the Boys"

After a few days in the kitchen I knew the ropes and gained some liberty within the limits of the big camp. A ring of sentries surrounded the place at night. They had savage dogs to aid them in their duties. More than a hundred Filipinos were employed at more or less slave labor within the camp, and I soon found messengers to the outside. I could not make contact with Captain Barnett and was afraid that he had been captured. Finally I did receive a message from the "Boys in the Hills," asking if I could steal ammunition from the American quartermaster's warehouse inside the post and smuggle it outside.

Food supplies for the Japs, kitchen utensils, all sorts of things were stored in the warehouse. I made frequent trips to it in my duties as K.P. By stealth and caution I was able to trickle out about two hundred bandoliers of cartridges during my stay at the camp. I got it outside the post by concealing it under empty sacks in the rear of the truck when I accompanied Nips on daily trips to farms and vegetable gardens. If I got no opportunity to drop it off at designated spots, I would sweat and wait for a try the next day.

A Friendly Nip Corporal

With me to Baguio had gone quite a quantity of my mimeographed anti–Jap papers, which I managed to pass out through reliable Filipinos.

Dr. Yamamoto, still friendly, introduced me to a Nip corporal. His name was the very common one of Nishi. He had been in California as interpreter for an export firm. His stateside slang was zippy and a proud accomplishment. He was purchasing agent for the hospital and would often pick me to accompany him. I no longer had any connection with the hospital and was quartered in a garage. Besides the trips after vegetables, I got into Baguio and nearby Trinidad often enough to make acquaintances with Filipinos.

Corporal Nishi gave me considerable freedom in town if no officers were in sight. I often accompanied him into stores. I got to needing a warm garment, for the mountain nights were pretty cool. I bought a cheap light sweater for ten pesos and when I got home I found the money wrapped with the jacket. Such incidents were always happening. A girl of Italian extraction who ran a fruit stand in the Baguio city market would not take my money for a dozen bananas. I told her to at least act as if she were accepting it as a pair of Nips were watching us. I put the fifty centavo note against her palm, intending to draw my hand away instantly. She squeezed my fingers and smiled and said, "Thee sees payment enough for me, Joe." The Nips saw the play and started toward us. She shook a finger in their faces and defiantly patted my cheek and said, "Come back tomorrow, Joe, for more bananas."

Low Down on the Nips

Filipino friends of mine from Fernando came to Baguio and sent me word by grapevine that they wished to see me. The only way to make the contact was through Nishi. I told him the situation. "You chiseler!" he said, and grinned and took me to town. We met my friends. He took us all to the back room of a cafe and stood guard outside while we visited. The friends gave me food and soap and other articles which were getting very scarce in the Islands. Nishi did not chip in for a share.

The corporal helped me in acquiring his language. He told me he longed to become an American citizen. He never treated me as other than a good friend, and he helped me when I got into trouble with other Japanese. This was in contrast to treatment I received from some of his countrymen for three long years.

Two young privates strolled up to where I was chopping wood behind the kitchen, for a talk. I could carry on in Japanese fairly well by now. The boys grew friendly and sympathetic with me. They told me the old story of buck privates in almost any man's army — how they disliked their officers, their warlords, and the war. We squatted and drew picture talk in the dust about the Battle of Bataan. They said that in the fighting there they got caught in the crossfire of Jap and Yank artillery. Their buddies were being blown to pieces. They put their arms around each other like two schoolgirls, lay on the ground and cried, and prayed they would not be killed or even sent against American doughboys.

This was the brave, self-sacrificing Jap soldier when stripped of the false pride and bravado built up by the myths of the samurai and Bushido. True, they were young and simple and unhardened.

There were other kinds of Japanese. Ogishee, for instance, a patient in the hospital. He became friendly and taught me many new words. I suggested to him that we could make some money selling radio parts from the post station to the Filipino black market. We would steal the stuff together, or sometimes he would bring it to me. I paid him ten pesos for each haul. What I was doing with the parts was getting them to the "Boys in the Hills," but to give Ogishee his due, he never knew that.

Jap Jazz Rumors

Word began to go the rounds in Camp John Hay concerning the future of us Yank prisoners. In order to get Americans still at large to surrender, the Nips were spreading talk that when all were rounded up we would be taken to Japan and sent home through an international arrangement for the exchange of prisoners. When I questioned my Nip friends about what their newspapers were saying on the subject they brought papers and pointed to articles. Later, when I could read the papers in Japan, I found that these items referred to the diplomatic exchanges arranged with our country. At that time, though, our sick and dying men were buoyed by a hope that was a certainty in their minds that we would all soon be sent home. Home! What a word that became!

Through grapevine I learned that the American prisoners at Camp O'Donnell had been transferred to another prison camp, Cabanatuan, where living conditions were reported to be greatly improved. After being away from them so long, I was eager to see old comrades, curious to know how they were faring and to learn what had happened to them.

About this time my old, fat pal, Sergeant-Major Fokunika of the San Fernando hospital, turned up. He had been on a visit to Cabanatuan. He was jelly-shaking with enthusiasm about how well his people were treating my people there, saying the boys weren't doing much work and that they had a jazz band organized. His picture of prison life sounded like home on the range, and because I was being treated pretty well here, I though perhaps the Japs had scored a change of heart and were treating all captives the same way.

I put another bug in greedy Ogishee's ear. A ten-peso bill was more than he got as his army pay in a month. A nice bright one sent him to looking up office papers to see what my future might be. Early in August he reported to me that all Americans would be started to Japan around September 25, 1942, and that all of them now ill in the hospital would be transferred to Cabanatuan within a few days.

His crystal ball reading proved to be sound. August saw nearly all prisoners who were unable to work — the sawmill victims particularly — off to the camp farther south. But Sergeant Macejewski, the ex–Foreign Legion man, and I and a few others were kept to continue our kitchen drudgery. Ogishee insisted that I would be sent to Japan and on home within a few weeks. I was afraid not to believe this.

Corporal Nishi also was poking about for dope on me. He said he just could not find anything definite. He gave me much advice on how to get along if I was taken to his home country. Dr. Yamamoto asked me if my health was good and whether I would like to "take a boat ride." He said he was going to try to keep me in Baguio as he had a tip-off that conditions at Cabanatuan were not what Dame Rumor was insinuating — in which he was correct, quite.[9]

Chopsticks for the Dead

My opinion of favorable Jap treatment underwent a change. It appeared that guerrilla activity had picked up to an intensity that worried the Nips. An American arriving at John Hay told me the enemy was being sniped like quail in the country farther north. He said that practically all the Americans camouflaged in Nip helmets and clothing, with whom I had traveled for a while, had been unwittingly picked off by the hidden gunners. Also, plenty of Japs.

To put oil on the guerrilla fire, some daring cuss raised the American flag over a hotel in downtown Baguio. It stayed there all night and half the day, winking colorfully in the breeze, before the Japs got courage to tear it down. I heard they hesitated for fear of a booby trap. They brought in planes to use against the free jungle fighters. In retaliation for bush-whacker activity the Nips began confiscating civilian property in the scene of action and were beating people occasionally, even on Baguio streets. That was the Japanese system, taking petty revenge.

One afternoon when we kitchen flunkies had finished our work and gone to our garage quarters for some siesta, three slain Jap soldiers were placed on boxes just outside our door. They had been shot dead-center between the eyes, the work of some East Texas squirrel hunter, likely as not. Exultation surged up in me that the "Boys in the Hills" were evidently not wasting the ammunition I had sent out.

Lighted candles were set at the dead men's heads and the typical Shinto death rites were begun. Offerings of fruit, fish and other delicacies surrounded the bodies. Bowls of steaming rice were placed close and chopsticks were stuck into the mouths of the corpses.

Japanese from all over the camp walked past to see their dead brothers-in-arms. In the procession came Captain Masatoku. Remember? The officer at Laganingalang who had been to the Texas Centennial and who I thought had been a spy. The man against whom I went cold and returned the compliment.

Masatoku saw us Americans standing there looking on curiously. He spoke to fellow officers. Suddenly they were rushing at us with threatening cries. We gave back into the garage. They snarled at us that their dead lay outside there because a stubborn and wicked American captain was in the hills inciting the Filipinos and stirring up trouble. I wanted to bellow, "Hooraw!" Captain Masotoku saw me. He stared, remembered, and shouted, whereupon the several officers began slapping at me, crowding one another to get to me. Finally I fell into a corner. They bent over me, asking if I was sorry. I got up and said "No" into their teeth. At that I was hauled outside the sleeping room into the main part of the garage. I thought of a lynching.

The Torture

Among many vehicles I was lifted, or tossed, up into a truck. Two rough soldiers drew my arms behind me, and up and over a studding, and tied them. The truck was pushed from under me. I dangled there by my arms. My legs were tied to the wheel of another truck. I was up in the air like an angel flying at a forty-five degree angle. I expected nothing except to be jerked by the truck and my arms pulled off.

It was comparative relief to see boxes placed under my feet and lighted candles from the dead Nips set on the boxes. They were only going to torture me with fire. In a moment I smelled scorching skin, but there wasn't much pain. When beri-beri numbs the feet there isn't much feeling. I just clamped my eyes on the studding next over and stared.

A great many Japanese had crowded in to see the fun. They jabbered and laughed. A few frightened Filipinos — I noticed once when I dropped my glance — stood sorrowing on the outer fringe. When the candles did not make me squirm and twist, glowing cigarettes were held up against my sagging belly. I had to grit my teeth, then, to keep from yelling.

I had seen both Americans and Filipinos punished by these brutal people. If they could make a victim cry out and squeal and curse they would keep up their torture until he was dead or practically so. The Japs kept hollering their derisive "*Koora*" and spitting at me, but I kept my jaws clamped.

Possibly the smell of burning skin got the best of them in the sweating, crowding throng. Also I imagine that Captain Masatoku feared reprimand from superior officers for disabling a prisoner capable of working. He abruptly ordered them to release me. He was worried when I stood again on the floor, but he knocked me down in farewell.

A Filipino who had witnessed the torture came to my aid immediately. He told me the prattling Nips had said I was a Christian — meaning in contrast to Shintoism, Buddhism or Mohammedanism — and therefore I was immune to torture, and that to continue might bring them bad luck. This may have been merely an excuse, as many Americans were tortured, but I may have brought them bad luck. Masatoku and all his associates here belonged to an outfit that was long later wiped out on Leyte.

And I'm still alive and my feet are in good condition.

A Bit of Sherlocking

One night two Jap army trucks loaded with American medical supplies were left in the garage where I slept. I always tried to find out where loaded trucks were going, then get word to reliable Filipinos who would carry it outside. It was easy to laugh and joke with the truck drivers, who were always asking me to make adjustments on sparkplugs or carburetors — which might or might not pep up their motors after I got through!

I never asked directly, "Where are you headed for, honorable soldier?" I would try the subtle approach like any correspondence school detective, such as: "Is it raining much in Lubagan now?" or "Any pretty girls up around Vigan?" They would come back, perhaps, with "Oh, the only trips I make are to Bontoo." Sometimes the unsuspecting farm-serfs from the homeland would even draw a map on the ground to show me, a stupid American, just exactly where they were taking supplies.

Those two medicine trucks must have been captured by our Boys in the Hills on my tip-off, because a few days later I was given two large jars of pink, sugar-coated quinine tablets of a kind I had seen on one of the trucks. These jars with some other medicine were sneaked in to me by grinning Filipinos. Since there were not many of our people in the hospital just then, I got the boys to take half the tablets out to the camp near Baguio where American and European civilians were interned. I had heard reports that these people were not receiving the best treatment in the world.

White-Skinned Women

On the frequent trips into town to market, I had seen Americans and other white-skinned men and women on the streets accompanied by Jap guards with pistols. The only communication with them was a nod or howdy-do gesture of the hand. Several times I saw two attractive young women, whether English or American I do not know. If their guard wasn't too close they would wave or give me a humorous wink. Once I found myself elbow to elbow with them in the market. We talked from the sides of our mouths like conventional convicts:

"Hello, why aren't you in our civilian camp?" one asked.

"I'm a soldier," I mumbled in reply.

"You?" they said together, staring at me.

I must not have looked my age. Their eyes said, "Liar."

Often two Italian boys came to me where I sat swinging my legs at the rear of our vegetable truck — little chaps with big grins, asking me in sign language why I didn't escape. They would point toward certain hills and make running motions with their none-too-clean hands. It seemed that every street urchin knew more about the technique of escape than the Japs.

We Move at Last

By the middle of September it was definite that we were to be moved, though "Where?" was the high-priced question. Corporal Nishi said I was going to Japan. He and his buddies envied me. Ah, Japan! Home where their pretty sisters and cousins lived. A beautiful land. A wonderful climate. Cherry blossoms in the spring. From their ravings I perhaps half believed I would find civilized people and better living arrangements for prisoners. Maybe these field soldiers were just a little harder than their folks at home.

Then moving orders came. Nishi gave me a farewell meal. He had managed to steal American food from the captured warehouses — sweet canned milk, corned beef, chocolate, and canned peaches.

I left Baguio with no regrets but with my clothing and few possessions packed with smuggled medicines, including the jar of pink quinine pills. I was on a truck with about twenty other American prisoners. One was Sergeant Macejewski, in better physical condition now. One or two were survivors of the march past the town of Laganingalang who had missed being shot under their Jap helmets. Some were captured guerrillas. A Lieutenant Ross, a flier who had been forced to work in Camp Hay apart from the others, was the ranking Yank in the party.

We kept to the truck until we arrived at Damortis, where we were loaded into boxcars along with Nip guards. There was no crowding; we had plenty of room and air. The guards sat in the doorways. I stood behind two of them and watched the countryside go by. From that position I witnessed one of the greatest pieces of impudence of my life when the train stopped at Tarlac.

A Charlie Chaplin

A tall, muscular, and darkly shining Moro from the southern islands came along the station platform. He wore a white turban, white duck clothing, and was as debonair as any idler about town. He was eating a banana. As I first glimpsed him he was peeling it down in four strips. He bit off half of the fruit, ate it at one swallow. He squeezed the remaining peel between thumb and finger and tossed the rest of the fruit into his mouth. Then in the best Charlie Chaplin manner he tossed the peel into the air and batted it with his hand, without even a glance at our Jap guards. The banana skin slapped one of them flat in the face with the swat of a wet rag.

A few steps farther on Mr. Moro stopped, did a perfect military about-face, and came back past. This time he rolled an amused eye at the Japs. The guard who had been banana-pasted whipped out his pistol in a fury to shoot the Mohammedan, but the other guard held his hand and warned that Moros were extremely dangerous people who might run amok or go *"Juramentado"** at the slightest provocation and kill everyone in sight with a curly kris. That cooled the man's ardor for revenge quickly.

*A Moro custom by which a heaven filled with beautiful young virgins can be gained through wrapping oneself tightly with bandages and proceeding to kill as many non–Mohammedan persons as possible before dying in the conflict.

CHAPTER IV

Cabanatuan and Bilibid Prisons

Our train rattled along almost to Manila in order to switch to a track leading to the Cabanatuan prison camp. At a village where we stayed overnight kindly Filipinos passed food to us in the cars. It was the last egg and ham I ate for nearly three years.

At the gate of dreaded Cabanatuan the next day we were searched perfunctorily by the Japanese guards, who missed my drugs; and by American officers down to our last seams. The Americans pounced on to my precious quinine as if it were pink pearls. They said it would be sent to the prison hospital. Men were dying by the scores of malaria and dysentery. So far as I could determine by a private investigation, my quinine never reached the prison hospital but was used by the officers who had malaria.

Because I was stronger than most I was grabbed at once for a grave-digging and burial detail. An American lieutenant was always in charge, and usually there was a chaplain. About forty were dying daily at this time, early October 1942. Chaplain Alfred Oliver, after liberation, briefly reported the situation there in an American magazine. He said[1]:

> Treatment by the Japanese of the sick American prisoners of war was as criminally brutal as Cabanatuan as at O'Donnell. Some 2,700 American prisoners of war lie buried at Camp No. 1. During July 1942, over 750 died there. Practically every death was the result of Japanese starvation and failure to provide the sick with medicine needed. The most pitiful incident of this period was the death of 135 American of diphtheria. American doctors had to stand impotently by and watch these helpless men choke to death. They died in horrible agony because the Japanese refused to supply the necessary anti-toxin, although it was in a storehouse one hundred yards away.

This was equally true in the hundreds of malaria deaths due to the lack of quinine which the Japanese had on hand and refused to supply to our doctors.

The graves we dug were shallow and wet, between two and three feet deep with water seeping in from the swamp soil to our knees. Crews carried the bodies, more or less naked, a kilometer across the plains and grasslands. Because it took so much work by the weakened men to dig separate graves, holes large enough for twenty bodies were scooped out of the muddy ground. The bodies were dropped in without benefit of coffins or cover. The chaplains would do their best to make it a Christian funeral. Crude crosses were set up and records were kept.

I disliked to touch the unbathed and emaciated bodies. I would pull handfuls of grass for gloves to grip necks and shanks with. Sometimes I had to look twice to see whether there was skin on the bone. We were always worked under pressure — by the time twenty or so were buried there would be as many more. They piled up on us sometimes, back at the camp.

Dysentery patients were kept isolated behind a fence at the so-called hospital. Medical men who tried to care for them deserve the Congressional Medal of Honor. The prison population was suffering from all sorts of disease and bad conditions, malnutrition, lack of sanitation, and lack of shelter. The buildings were mostly of nipa or sawale siding, and thatch, with shelves inside to lie on. I sometimes wondered why it wouldn't be more humane for the Nips or our own men to ease the helpless and hopeless sufferers out of their misery. Of course that just isn't done. Only a small percentage of the sick ever recovered. If they got over their sickness they were in many instances worked to death.

Blood-Brother Groups

Four American officers were caught one evening in an attempt to escape. They had almost reached a point where they could crawl under the fence by way of a sewage drain. At this time the Nips had the prisoners divided into "blood-brother groups" of ten, so that if one escaped and was not recaptured his nine "brothers" were executed. These four officers, two of them colonels, were locked up for a couple of days; then we saw them marched outside the fence and shot. I witnessed it with my own eyes.

An American Indian boy who had managed to slip away from Cabanatuan had hidden in a nearby village, passing himself off for a native. He obtained work in a Japanese warehouse. He married a Filipino girl. No one was wise to the situation. He was in the clear until his wife began listening to Jap propaganda. They were telling the Filipinos to "come forward and confess your sins" and the honorable Japanese army would forgive them. The Indian's wife, to get her husband free of all danger, talked him into confessing. He was promptly taken back to Cabanatuan and beaten until he swelled all over. He was marched around the camp with a sign around his neck saying, "It is impossible to escape." After that jolly hike he was strapped to a post and made to stand under the tropical sun day after day, a punishment that drove men insane. He was still there when I left.

Two companies of Jap recruits training for camp duty guarded the fence. They took a stroll in formation to a nearby village and marched back singing, with the long-haired bloody head of a Filipino dangling from a string through the ear and tied to a bamboo pole. They set this relic up at the main gate as a warning to Filipinos who might be thinking of giving assistance to a POW in any manner.

It was at Cabanatuan that my friend Henry Lee wrote his verses and hid them beneath the floor of a nipa hut. These verses were dug up when Lieutenant Colonel Henry A. Mucci led his 6th Ranger Infantry Battalion far behind Japanese lines on Luzon in a daring raid, and liberated the American prisoners of war from Cabanatuan on the night of January 30, 1945. Lieutenant Lee's verses were found written on a brown paper composition book, wrapped in six layers of rotting canvas. The book, frayed and dirty, its pages smudged by sweat and the author's painstaking erasures, contained a total of thirty-six poems. According to all information available, my friend Henry was one of the prisoners of war who lost their lives when a Japanese prison ship was bombed off Formosa on January 9, 1945 — a scant twenty-one days before they would have been liberated had they not been snatched from Cabanatuan. Some of Lee's poems were published by the *Saturday Evening Post*.

Lieutenant Lee stood by the prison fence one day where we were watching an execution. He remarked bitterly to me as I stood beside him, "Those barbaric sons of bitches!" Later he expressed his sentiments in his poem, "An Execution," published in the *Saturday Evening Post* in June 1946.

Officers Run Racket

Food at Cabanatuan consisted of the eternal rice and a sickening soup of green weeds and water. Our captors knew there was plenty of money hidden in the camp, and men who had it would purchase food from the outside. At one time American officers put out the order that an enlisted man could possess only ten or fifteen pesos. Any excess cash had to be turned in to a "collecting committee." Members of this group disgraced themselves for life for so swindling their helpless fellows, for it was nothing but a racket. A few responsible officers did not tolerate it for long, but they were in the minority. Most of the officers at Cabanatuan must have been poor specimens of men to begin with.

Even men of good character and honesty before the war weakened and became unreliable under such revolting conditions as prevailed at the camp. Men lost their minds. One dying hospital patient made a rush for the fence but was stopped by our men before the Japs could shoot him. After that we had to keep a walking guard of our own inside the fence at all hours, day and night, by orders of the Nips. I pulled guard duty one night, walking post four hours and resting two. The next day I was too exhausted to help bury the dead. That's how men were at Cabanatuan.

While at Cabanatuan hospital one afternoon I looked across the fence of the dysentery isolation pen and saw the shrunken face of another of my Indian friends, from Santo Domingo Pueblo in New Mexico. I slipped him the only sulfa drugs I possessed, three tablets of the precious medicine. These pills were being sold for the equivalent of about $350, American money, for each tablet at that time. The Domingo boy lived through his dysentery and imprisonment. Years later his people presented me with a handmade silver and turquoise concho belt at a ceremony in New Mexico where other Bataan men and I were being awarded the Bataan Medal by the governor of the state.

Bilibid

About the middle of October, when I had been at Cabanatuan eight or ten days — it is impossible to remember exactly — I was ordered into a formation and marched to the railroad station with about ninety-nine other men. It was ten kilometers under a broiling sun to the tracks, and we were marched at a fast hep-he-hep. As I had been swindled of all my hundreds of pesos I sold a shining bright compass, which I had held onto by good luck, and got a few coins with which to buy some needed food in the confusion at the station. This would not have been needed had the Nips let us accept food offered by the Filipinos.

We arrived in Manila late in the evening. This beautiful city, which I had so loved to visit before the war, somehow looked deserted. For the first time in ten months I saw electric street lights and signs. We marched past a nightclub where an orchestra was playing the Missouri Waltz. We glimpsed men and women in evening clothes. We caught the scent of perfumes and fresh flowers. It was a reminder that there were still places left where disease, death and misery were not rampant. I swore to myself that I would survive and see comfortable life again. I repeated General MacArthur's words, "I shall return."

Life or Death

We were placed in a large cellblock in the old Philippine prison of Bilibid. So desperate were the Japs for metal that the steel bars had been taken from the windows and replaced with wooden ones. For a few days we were in suspense as to whether we were to be executed or sent elsewhere. A group of twenty captured Filipino guerrillas were thrown in with us. They told a story of hardships. With the rainy season on, Japs taking all rice and food supplies, lack of ammunition, and cholera wiping out whole villages, it had been impossible to continue their resistance.

In this great prison many of the inmates not physically fit were men who had been wounded seriously or lost limbs on Bataan and Corregidor. One thing was in our favor — plenty of water for bathing. Filipinos occasionally tossed food over the walls to us. I was able to send a message to Rosalina and receive a reply.

After about a week in Bilibid the dreaded tropical dysentery hit me. Then one day—I'm not certain about time in those last days—we in our block were counted off, one on this side, one on that, as in choosing up sides for a game at school. It seemed to be an "eenie meeinie, minie, mo" system until I saw that the officers had papers from which they were picking our names. Execution? Work? From the frowns of the Japs selecting us it appeared to be the former. It was. The men in the group opposite from me were herded into a corner of the prison wall. A single Jap enlisted man raised a submachine gun and riddled them with bullets until his gun was empty! Men in my group fainted as we watched the horrible scene, believing that we would be slaughtered that way in a few moments. We were forced to throw our dead comrades into a deep hole in the prison yard and other prisoners appeared to cover them over with trash and dirt!

CHAPTER V

Prison Ship to Japan

My counted-off group was marched out of Bilibid. I could barely hold up my head as we were herded through the Manila streets. Where were we going? The answer seemed obvious when we reached the port area and saw ships, but the sight did not make me feel any better. Late in the afternoon we were herded on to a small cargo ship named *Nagato Maru*. It was a boat with four hatches into the holds. About fourteen hundred prisoners went on board. We had to descend on ladders into the belly of the ship. Some of us could barely make it down the rungs. One or two dropped into the middle hatch where I had descended. We found ourselves on coal. We were in coal bunkers.

A thousand or so Jap soldiers tramped on board. They kept to the upper and deck spaces where there was air and visibility. There in the bunker the iron sides of the vessel were so hot from the tropical sun that steam rose when men urinated against the metal. We began to bake. The stench of filth and rotting vegetables tossed down on the coal before we arrived was in our nostrils. There was no movement of fresh air into the steel box.

It was dusk when the ship turned loose from the dock and began to slide through Manila Bay. It was the first day of November 1942. The hold was still hot, and was stinking now from the sweat and sickness of the packed men. I had to get more air. *Had to*! I pushed and fought my way through the touchy men to the straight-up-and-down cleat ladder. I managed to climb it to deck level. How marvelous is a breath of clean air! I could see the calm and gracious water of the bay. In the moonlight were other ships; we were in a convoy. A Jap officer saw me and knocked my hold on the rung and I dropped down on the coal. I struggled my way back to my pack of rags against a steel wall.

It turned out that there was one latrine for nearly three thousand men. A good many could not climb the ladder to reach it. Five gallon gasoline cans were lowered by ropes into the holds for the disposal of waste.

I managed to sleep some of that night, despite men stumbling or crawling over me. I was too sick and weak from dysentery to curse them. In the morning, pails of rice and soup were lowered to us, as to hyenas in a pit. I cared little whether I ever ate again. Then I remembered my resolve and the word pounded me on the back — survive, survive, survive. I got up by pulling on the wall. I pushed myself away from it. I fought my way to food. Officers were making an effort to apportion it equally into our cups. Oddly, it turned out that with a cup of rice and soup in my hand I had an appetite. I fairly gulped the mixture.

China Sea Graveyard

After about a week in that hellhole, and against all probabilities, I began to recover from the dysentery. I wasn't the only sick man on board, though from the "I's" that I have been using it might appear so. Hundreds were sick and suffering. Nobody, I think, was completely free from maladies or moods. Lieutenant Dornberger of Kansas, who was to become a good friend, was lying close by me, a sufferer from beri-beri, and quite as weak and ill as I. Captain Leslie Doane, likewise from Kansas, who was to be with me for a long time, cared for the lieutenant, bringing food or helping him over the coal to the filth cans.

The ship's black gang began to use the coal for their steam and sometimes it would shift under us.

With the diminishing of the dysentery I was able to move about some. Men died every day from dysentery, malaria, malnutrition and various other ailments including despair. I became able to help lower the bodies over the side and drop them with a splash into the China Sea. It made me remember my indignation and care in the burial of the Grumbler. Perhaps it was better that these men died early; it saved them from longer suffering.

Sometimes in the earlier part of the voyage we were allowed to linger on the deck in the latrine line shuffle. Late one afternoon when we were in this slow-time fidget the lookout cried from the bridge, "*Sensuikan!*" A wild shout went up all over the ship. Americans began to yell, "It's a submarine! It's a Yank! It's ours!" I don't know how they knew, if they did, until the Japs' single 75-millimeter piece, tied to the deck with ropes, began to roar out its shells. The Japs rushed about in their usual confusion, frantically driving us back to the holds. I got butt-slugged* a couple of times just to speed me along.

It was hard to go back into the coal-hold and leave the sunshine and that battle, with the possibility of an American-made tinfish hitting and sinking us. The ship just behind us was sunk. I didn't see it, but the story was told too persistently to be a fake. After that we were allowed no more time on deck while at sea.

White Strangers on Formosa

Two weeks on the China Sea put us in at Takao on Formosa Island. We were allowed occasionally to go on deck, and some men were taken ashore to help the Nips load supplies. All men in my hold were ordered out and more coal was loaded in with conveyor buckets. A small breeze blew the black dust across us. There was no water to wash it off. We got a lot of laughs at our looks — those who could still laugh.

The Japanese told us we were the first white men allowed to put in on Formosa in thirty years. At night we saw anti-aircraft searchlights walking the sky and we practically prayed for a raid by American planes. We saw white Japanese ships with hospital red crosses pained conspicuously on them being loaded with ammunition and guns.

Then we pulled out for Japan. Three days out of Takao a storm arose and the captain put into a small island harbor. The little hunk of land had been swept by typhoons until not a tree or wisp of grass remained on the desert surface. There were a small landing strip for planes and two crude buildings. The sea was still rough when we went on. More men were dying all the time and were dropped over the side into water that was growing colder and colder.

Our food and water supplies were shortened until we were about

---

*Beaten with the wooden stock of a rifle.

to die of thirst, hunger and restlessness. We discovered that seven of our officers had taken for themselves part of the water and food assigned to our hold. During the night these seven officers were strangled to death by other prisoners and the next day thrown overboard into the icy waters without a word of prayer or regret. Such was my experience on a Japanese prison ship in the twentieth century.*

*For a similar detailed account of another Japanese Hell Ship the reader is referred to Ira C. Wolfert, "Lest We Forget," *The Reader's Digest*, April 1945, pp. 57–61.

CHAPTER VI

Slave at Yodogawa

As we neared Japan we no longer suffered from the heat. It was the other way around: cold. Damnably cold for us in our rags of tropical clothing. I had only my two pairs of shorts — one, the Victory pants — and a thin Filipino army jacket. I had borrowed a pair of new leather shoes from a legless prisoner in Bilibid but they were as cold as saddle leather in January without socks. The change of climate gave men colds and dripping beaks. It was in this happy state that we landed in Japan at the port of Moji on Kyushu Island on Thanksgiving Day, November 26, in the year of our Savior 1942.

We were herded off the ship to a windy dock in spitting snow. As we stepped from the gangplank we were wetted with disinfectant from head to foot. Our rags were flapping in the wind. Snow was freezing on our faces. Men shook so from the cold that they could hardly stand.

God, it was cold! The memory is still so sharp that as I write this on April 2, 1948, at five o'clock in the afternoon in Texas, I get up and shift my typewriter nearer to a cozy, simmering gas stove. I did not get warm in Japan until the next summer.

Dripping disinfectant, we were each handed a small wooden placard with a number painted on it in black. These we hung around our necks — a new dog tag. By chance Corporal Nick Metta of New York was handed No. 1 and I got No. 2, for the group we had been quickly herded into. The division into groups was quickly accomplished but we did not move to shelter. Instead we were ordered to squat there on the wind-blown dock and open our bundles for customs inspection. There were five inspectors for the hundreds of men. They kept together. They looked at and put a rubber stamp on everything we had. The packs of junk we carried were worthless even to us, for the most part, valuable mostly for hiding letters and pictures from home, or any money we might have left. The inspectors appeared to be particularly concerned with Filipino cigarettes and American playing cards.

Hours passed and the Nips offered us no food for our hungry bellies, nor supplied any stimulant-medicine to the muscle-jerking wretches that we were. With my seat on the cold concrete I honestly believed I would freeze to death. I believed exactly that. I rubbed my arms and legs frantically to keep up circulation. But I would survive if I could. Men squirmed and twisted and cursed and moaned. We must have looked like human maggots wiggling in refuse.

When at last the ragman's holiday search of our possessions was finished, they began rechecking the groups of one hundred, counting and shifting us according to our physical condition for work — not for hospitalization. I thought it would never, never end, but a change did come when an interpreter came to my group, looked at our wooden dog tags, and informed Corporal Metta and me that as Nos. 1 and 2, we would have command of the group. He put bands around our arms with Japanese characters on them.

The Freezing Continues

Three other groups of one hundred men were moved near ours and we were told to move off in formation. Corporal Metta croaked commands. My last glance back at the ship showed two of my acquaintances being brought down the gangplank on stretchers. They were laid on that windy dock. I never saw them again.

Other blocks of four hundred fell into the march. A tall, strict, German-trained Jap lieutenant named Yamada was in charge of the column. He howled at us, and his assistants kept knocking down both prisoners and Jap soldiers indiscriminately when things didn't snap along fast enough. As we hurried along the street — if hungry, stumbling, half-naked, bone-chilled men could hurry — Master Sergeant Miller of Illinois stumbled along behind me. He could hardly keep up. I put my arm around him to assist. I thought it strange that a man twice my age should have tears in his eyes, but I suppose he was suffering mightily. He died within two weeks.

One man fell to the ground and Corporal Draper, a Marine from Salt Lake City, picked him up and carried him across his shoulder. Lieutenant Dornberger's feet were so swollen from beri-beri that he stumped along like a man with no feet at all.

After plenty of this, we arrived at another dock and boarded a ferry boat and crossed the water separating Moji from Shimonoseki. It was colder than ever and the snow was still spitting at us. In the streets of Shimonoseki we marched to a railway station, where we were loaded into third-class passenger cars with wooden seats. But every man had the blessing of a seat. How grateful we were for that. With doors and windows closed, the heat of our bodies warmed the air somewhat. We saw steam pipes and got to nosing around, and someone discovered how to turn the steam on. The car warmed up and eventually we stopped shivering and could relax a little.

Japan from Car Window

Japs came in with a small box of boiled rice and another very small box containing fish, orange, pickled vegetables, seaweed and onion. Each man got a tiny pinch of each of those edibles, not half a bite. Although this was the first and best meal the Japanese home army ever gave us, it was so little that I could have gulped it all in two and a half swallows.

Corporal Metta and I sat together listening to the guard telling us over and over that we were leaders. The shades were down and we were not supposed to look out at the country. I did a little peeping but darkness came and I went to sleep, despite flat car wheels, and did fancy shuteye most of the night.

In the morning we were fed the same scanty dole. The wrinkles slightly out of my stomach, I meandered to the rear of the car. The door had no shade. As we were the last car of the train I could take in the landscape. Neat fields were flowing past. They were jammed right up within inches of the rails. Japan has to be economical with its land because the population is so dense. When we rumbled through villages with their crowded-together, doll-size clapboard houses, I looked for familiar signs. In every foreign country I had been in I had seen the familiar Coca-Cola and Dr. Lyon's toothpowder signs, but my eyes searched vainly for them in Japan.

The Japs discovered that we had the steam heat turned on and valved it off with warning orders. It grew cold in the coach again; our bushy beards were about the warmest coverings we had and they weren't long enough yet to cover our backs. We were an unholy sight, typical more-or-less-despised prisoners of war. But my increasing curiosity kept my thoughts off my looks and miseries.

Arrival in Osaka

At about three o'clock in the afternoon we rolled into the city of Kobe and were given another cold and windy march to the streetcars. They took us to the dirty slum and factory district of the nearby indus- trial city of Osaka, which was to be the hometown for most of us who survived, for two and a half years — for me until I was sentenced to the coal mines for sabotage.

Here we had another shivering stroll of about a mile to a run-down factory, the Yodogawa Steel Works, located in the northwest section of Osaka's manufacturing district.

The plant covered several blocks, possibly one hundred acres; I don't know how much. There were many black and dingy buildings, large and small, as I found out in time, housing two foundries, two steel work- shops, a huge steel rolling mill, a helmet factory, storage buildings, ware- houses, cooling ovens, mess halls, a gasoline drum factory, offices, a bolt and nut mill, piles of steel and sand and cinders, our POW barrack; and there were some small homes of native workers with their little vegetable gardens. The plant was on reclaimed land beside the Yodo River just where it emptied into Osaka Bay and met the sea tides. A seawall held back the river and tides. On three sides of us were canals usable by large vessels and barges. One canal ran through the middle of our grounds with a Japanese bridge arching over it. It was in addition to the other three canals and was Yodogawa's own water basin. A city road passed along one side, and the entire area was surrounded by a tight board fence a little higher than a tall American's head.

All of these things we were to learn gradually. Upon our arrival among the dirty, patched buildings the Japs lined us up according to rank on the larger of two cinder drill grounds. Thus it was found that there were commissioned officers in our group and Corporal Metta and I were relieved of our armbands. It turned out there were about thirty officers. Two were majors, William B. Reardon of Albuquerque, New Mexico, and John Martin of Alabama. The Japs ordered one of them to be our commanding officer, within prisoner limitations. The two stepped aside and conferred in low voices. Major Martin was the older and was suffering from beri-beri. Major Reardon, in better health, accepted the heavy responsibility of the group command, which probably even a brigadier would have hesitated over.

Our Civilian Bosses

Factory officials dressed in Western-style business suits, with their pants legs stuffed into wrap-leggings and with gold stripes around their hats to show rank — hats that looked like those of organ-grinders' monkeys — now gathered and looked us over like horses, probably discussing how much work they could get out of us on how little food. They seemed to take no thought whatever that we were freezing in our rags.

The water all around us made the damp area exceedingly cold. I could not see how any of us would survive six weeks in such a climate and such heartbreakingly dismal surroundings. Our spirits were at low ebb. I would have given an ear, actually, to be permitted to step behind a wall out of the wind.

Lieutenant Yamada, who had brought us here, interrupted the civilians to demonstrate that Americans could be knocked around and to show the bosses just how it was done. Blows on cold, stiff bodies hurt, and kicks hurt worse. After that show we were ordered to strip off our coats, or whatever scraps of rags and blankets we were using for coats, and lay all our possessions on the ground, where they were inspected for weapons. Many of us stood there in our bare backs. When that job was finished an interpreter read a paper to us, setting forth that in return for good wages, food, medical attention, and comfortable quarters we must sign our names to a paper promising not to attempt escape. A handful of others and myself avoided signing thanks to the milling around during the procedure, much to the confusion of the sons of heaven who were trying to find the delinquents. Finally, after being warned that we must obey the Japanese civilians as well as army personnel, bow to and salute every subject of the Emperor, we were sent into a huge foundry structure. This was a makeshift place, not the permanent barrack that we were to occupy two or three days later.

One Stove for 400 Men

The roof of the foundry was a hundred feet above our heads. We might as well have been outdoors except there wasn't so much wind inside. We received four blankets each, made of cotton and with about the protection of burlap; a hard pillow of rice straw; and, for eating utensils, a tiny bowl and chopsticks. We were served a meal of boiled rice and oats and a weak vegetable soup. When I speak of Japanese vegetable soup henceforth, I shall mean one single vegetable, as cabbage or turnip, boiled without salt or other seasoning. In all my imprisonment I rarely received more than a tablespoon of vegetable. It was the first attempt of many of the men to eat with chopsticks, and it was a laugh despite our shaking bodies.

After the meal I was interested in nothing but wrapping up in my blankets and trying to get warm. We weren't allowed to turn in, though, until we were lined up and counted three or four times more and were taught that it wasn't a Japanese custom to walk on floors with shoes. We had to stand barefooted on cold concrete until the guards were satisfied with the counting.

Only one man died that night. As I was putting my pocketbook under my hard pillow a guard snatched it. It held only a few pictures and other items worthless to him but he kept it. Next morning twenty or so men were unable to get up out of their blankets. The Japs supplied the necessary lift, with kicks. During the morning we asked for heat and were given one small coke-burning stove. It was impossible for four hundred men to warm by it. Because I was persistent and stronger than some, I managed to get fairly near the fire. It was exhausting though to stand and stand and be continually jostled. When someone complained to the guards of the cold they made amends — by taking us outside, making us strip to the waist on the smaller, nearer cinder patch and do calisthenics. I saw men with beri-beri so bad that the skin of their feet was about to burst from the swelling, made to run and jump on that cindery ground.

The second day we were informed that all officers must learn to speak Japanese and that enlisted men must learn to count to twenty and obey drill commands. Instruction pamphlets were passed out and we were marched to the cinders again. There the Jap drill sergeants took us in hand as if we were raw recruits. They shouted "*Kiotske, hidari, mike hidari, mae susume, tomarel!*"* until the poor half-dead prisoners were jerking about like puppets on strings. We got all out of formation and milled like cattle. Because I knew enough Japanese to understand, I was soon sent back to quarters. There, I was the only man present and had the stove to myself— and did I embrace it! I had just about soaked up a bellyful of heat when a Jap guard entered who did not know that I had been excused. He walked me at the point of his pistol to the cinders and made me chase myself in a circle until I dropped.

I caught myself wishing I had made more of an attempt to escape, back in the Philippines. But I choked off that thinking right quick; no use to handicap myself with wishful regretting. I just rekindled my determination to survive and someday see these stupid brutes suffer, too. Cold, it seems to me, is the most demoralizing agency.

Our New Osaka Home

The third day we were assigned to the room that was to be our home address for two and a half years. It was a second-floor space about forty by eighty feet, over a metal-working shop. Outside stairs let us up and down. At the foot of the stairs were the office, kitchen, washroom, and toilet and, just outside, the smaller cinder drill ground. Inside the big room, around the walls and through the middle, were shelves six feet deep. Actually they were platforms in two tiers, the first about two feet above the floor, the second about four feet above that. The top shelves were attained by climbing a cleat-ladder nailed to the roof-supporting

---

*Attention, left face, forward march, halt!

timbers. The shelves were our beds, our chairs, our resting places. We crawled onto them head first, slept with our heads inward and our feet out. Anyone passing could tickle our soles or smash our beri-beri toes with a fist. There were no partitions between the men. We slept there as cozily as hogs, elbow to elbow. Between the rows of shelves were low benches, not for seats but for serving food.

Sanitation facilities for nighttime, or for the sick who could not get down to the toilet adjoining the kitchen at the foot of the outside stairs, consisted of buckets in the narrow hall or passage that ran across the short way of the room. In that passage was one stove to warm that entire room. For ventilation there were two windows in each end of the room and a million holes in the old walls, some large enough to stick your fist through. The Japs opened the windows for a night or two and we as promptly closed them. Plenty of wind blew in anyhow. In summer we kept them open.

I Acquire a Buddy

By the time we got into our permanent quarters I had acquired a congenial friend, Sergeant Willis B. Minor of Missouri. He was an air forces mechanic and a man of character. We were to be together in work and escapades until I was sentenced to the coal mines and he was sent north in the spring of 1945.

Also the officers, ordered to learn Japanese and finding that I spoke it somewhat, replenished my treasury by passing money to me with which to try to contact the black market for extra food. The officers slept in the same room on the same shelves with the rest of us hogs.

During these exciting first days of freezing and fighting for the stove room and getting settled in our new home-sweet-home, the Japs classified us for their work. They asked for skilled mechanics. Sergeant Minor's hand went up and he gave me a sidewise kick on the leg and whispered fiercely:

"Tell 'em you're a diesel engineer!"

My hand shot up. I couldn't tell a diesel engine from an Irishman's pipe. But Minor had his reasons, and his tricks. Trust him for that, always. He knew that a machine shop was to be opened as soon as skilled labor could be obtained in a building near our barrack. It was to assemble diesel engines. The Japs stood us aside for that work. Minor grinned his gentle-jeering grin and told me that he had once in all his life torn down and put a diesel motor back together. I confessed that I had once done the same for a Model T Ford. So by Japanese records I am a diesel engineer, if any employer is seeking the same.

Labor in the Drum Factory

For the month before the shop opened I was assigned to a factory across the company's canal that was putting out metal gasoline drums, much like those we have in America. My 12-hours-a-day task was to stop a drum rolling toward me on a concrete floor, pick up a plug, put a rubber washer on it, screw the plug into the drum bunghole, lift up the drum two feet, set it on a chute, and give it a shove. Approximately five hundred drums a day rolled at me. They weighed perhaps forty or fifty pounds; I don't know how much. Moreover, they came to me from a water tank where they were tested for leaks. They were always wet. Besides, an inch or so of water accumulated daily on the floor. I was wet, too, my hands, sleeves, the front of my pants from the belt down. And it was a cold winter.

The job was easy compared to that of some prisoners, whom I could see out in the rain and wind loading trucks or carrying steel, hard labor that they had never done before in their lives. My feet, numb from beri-beri, did not suffer too much from the wet and cold; but as the disease grew rapidly worse, my soles would burn as if the floor were a furnace plate. Nor can I say that my back didn't have a crick in it by night. Occasionally I earned myself a slap for not working fast enough.

I have been asked by people here in America if that slapping wasn't hard to endure. It was, indeed. At first, anyhow. One can get used even to it. At first, though, men with tempers and nerves that they could not control got themselves terribly beaten or starved to death for fighting back. The men with the best self-control grimly took it and survived.

The Old Pirate Helps

I soon learned to get in some rest when guards or foremen were not present. The Jap civilian workers followed the same tactics and to hell with the war. My stomach was always shouting for food. That made barrel-lifting seem harder. I drank all the water I could hold to have something to lift the barrels against. One day I became so weak that I dropped to the floor. I was half-frozen too. A kindly old Japanese took me to a fire behind a stack of drums. He made a pot of hot tea for me. He was delighted when I thanked him in his own tongue.

At this time, in late 1942, food wasn't too hard to get or too closely rationed to the civilians; so the old man trudged away happily and brought me a bowl of rice and some fish from the factory-area cafeteria, for which I paid him. Later this old man, a familiar figure on the Yodogawa grounds, was called the Old Pirate by the Yanks because of a peg leg, scarred face, and the pipe he kept strapped in a leather case on his belt like a knife or pistol. As time went on he bought some food for me on the black market, but it was never enough.

One day the yellow-banded superintendent caught me loafing at the Old Pirate's fire and slapped me down. From then on I kept a wary eye out for the "Gold Stripers," as we called the bosses for the gold stripes on their hats. When the big boss got to watching for me around the old man's fire, the Pirate would take me on a pretended trip for barrel tops and I would be able to dry out and warm in front of a big blast furnace. We would stand there together in that fierce heat until our bones smoked.

Roll Call an Ordeal

In the first weeks only about one hundred of our four hundred men were working. The others were either too ill or were pretending to be. The army and factory officials seemed unable to agree as to how much food we needed to work on; so our underfeeding continued. Men who would not or did not work were issued only one-third of the daily ration. Men who were too sick to work were sure to die eventually of slow starvation. During that first winter we lost an average of two men a day, by death.

A prison work day started at 6 A.M., even for "experts" like Minor and me after we got started in the diesel shop. Jap guards would come running into our packed sleeping room with fixed bayonets and hollering "*Sho-sho,*" which meant to get out of your blankets and off your shelf in a hurry. Men who were slow were prodded with bayonets or bumped with rifle butts, even if sick. Sometimes an interpreter would intercede and argue with the guards to let the poor devils alone.

Often we would stand shivering for half an hour until Sergeant Hirose or one of his staff got around to counting us. When the fiery little sergeant entered the room, someone would holler "*Kiotske*" and we were supposed to snap to attention. Not the easy, relaxed attention of the American soldier but the rigid position of the Japanese with arms pasted stiffly down the sides like sticks.

Sick prisoners with the weak trembles could not jump to attention and hold the position like well-fed and trained soldiers, but the Japs demanded it anyhow. They frequently impressed us with the necessity of better line-ups by hauling slow-thinking, weak and weary men out of line and slapping them until they fell to the floor, then kicking them until they got up. We others had to stand helplessly and see or hear. That a man might be bleeding about the face concerned our heroic captors not at all; they just kept up their roughness until satisfied. At the last a beaten man might have a pail of cold water sloshed over him to snap him out of his laziness. That was great sport for the Nips; we could tell by the way they laughed. Back in line the victim would exert every atom of his willpower to stand at rigid attention. Then whatever noncom was in charge of the roll call would shout attention and at ease until we were executing the orders properly.

When finally we were all at sufficient rigidness to satisfy the noncom, each American at the end of a line would holler "*Tenko*" and the line would count off in Japanese: "*Ichi, ni, san, shi, go, roku.*"* When numbers got past twenty they became difficult and we would have to stand there counting until we got it correct. The men who nervously made mistakes got a slap to make them count right. With the guard in front of him ready to slap him again, the prisoner would make further mistakes and get more punishment.

Never See America Again

When roll call, "*Tenko*" in Japanese, was finished we still stood at attention while our barrack was inspected for cleanliness. What a par-

*One, two, three, four, five, six.

ody! When we moved into the room it was so dirty that a fire hose would not have cleaned it. But there were certain ways in which we had to arrange our so-called blankets and bowls and chopsticks. After tenko, orders for the day were read and frequently a little speech was added, which went about like this:

"If you do not work hard today you will be punished. You must obey our rules. You must be happy and healthy. You are all sick because you are not happy. But although we wish you to be happy you must not sing or whistle or smile, nor play while at work. You will never return to America, so you must adapt yourself to the Japanese way of living."

After this cheering little talk we would wash. The washroom was at the foot of the stairs. There was sufficient cold water, but the small space was crowded, for four hundred men. Washed and dried with whatever we had for towels, we would troop back upstairs for our first important ceremony of the day — breakfast.

The Animals Eat

One man from each sleeping section would be detailed to bring up our rice from the kitchen. Each prisoner set his empty bowl and soup container on the bench in front of him, then stood back while the KP moved along doling out daubs of sticky rice or pouring soup. Every eye watched greedily to see that the food was divided equally and no favoritism shown. Brawls would occur over the server's packing one bowl and merely tossing the gob lightly into another. Even one grain spilled on a bench would be picked up and eaten.

When all containers were filled each man would jump for his. Turn your eyes away for a second from your chow and it would be gone. Ethics did not prevail at eating time.

"What if a fellow were caught snatching, he'd have gobbled the food into his belly, so what could you do?" T'hell with honor, a guy might be dead before the next meal.

In our barrack, when the Japs weren't around, the officers could not enforce strict discipline, for they too were hungry and weak and fighting for life itself the same as us. The leadership and executive ability of the officers did not shine any brighter than that of the enlisted personnel. The enlisted men kept their honor as clean as the commissioned men, though they were forced to work harder. We all did things which we would be ashamed to tell about.

We were no longer quite men of civilized character but were more like animals fighting for survival. Yet none ever forgot that he was an American, and we tossed the monkey wrench into every Japanese cogwheel that we could find open.

Probably we at Yodogawa would have fared better had we cooperated with the Nips a little better at the beginning. We roused their antagonism. Inspecting officers would come and scold us for being the worst-behaved prisoner group, they said, in the Osaka area. They ranted that our living conditions were the worst and would be permitted to remain so because we were stubborn and troublesome. They hoped to reform us, perhaps, but we only smirked and were proud of our record of annoyance. We knew that surely no prison camp could be worse than ours in that winter of 1942–43, yet we were not going to be good boys and work hard for the Emperor just for a little more soup.

Packages from Canada

On Christmas Day 1942, we worked until evening as usual although we had been promised a holiday. However, on December 27 the workplaces were closed for the regular semimonthly Japanese rest day, "*yasume*" day. This was not a national custom but seemed to prevail in the Osaka factory area. In midafternoon Lieutenant Yamada — that German-trained Nip who had conducted us from the landing port — arrived and had us all lined up on our shelves and went down the lines giving every third man a box of Canadian Red Cross food. We had never dreamed of such a treat. As we clawed open the boxes and divided the delicacies, such as corned beef, butter, tea, sugar, jam, candy, we gabbled like a schoolhouse full of Christmas kids at home. My portion was enough to fill my belly and stop the feeling of hunger for the rest of the day. This was the first time I had not been hungry since leaving the Philippines nearly two months before. I crowed like a rooster and patted my stomach, and thought temporarily that the Japs weren't so bad after all. We were plain chow-happy.

And right here, while I am feeling good on memory, is a suitable place to speak of Lieutenant Yamada. At first we hated him for his harsh discipline, but in the two months he was with us as a visitor-inspector we came to respect him. He was honest. He was just. He'd as soon punish a Jap as an American. If he found a guard mistreating us unduly he would punish that guard. He saw that packages from outside were distributed to us. We regretted when he was transferred. Though not a kindly man, he had as many upright qualities as any officer I ever served under, whatever the nationality. He was a decided Japanese exception.

With the boxes of food disappearing and stomachs filled, we felt some of the spirit of Christmas in a heathen land. We sang "God Bless Canada."

The Japanese were a bit lenient with us around Christmas, not because they had any understanding of the event, but because it was close to their biggest holiday of the year, January 1.

We Kowtow to Emperor

By eight o'clock of the morning of January 1, 1943, no prisoner had been beaten and we decided we were going to have a swell time of it for one day at least, while the Japanese nation was observing the New Year. It was a double holiday for them. It was the birthday of the Emperor and every one of his subjects. A Jap does not have an individual birthday. He is as old as the number of years he had lived in. A baby born December 31 is two years old January 1, because he has lived in two calendar years, though actually he might not have been breathing a minute.

On this New Year morning all of us Yodogawa POW's were ordered to the cinder yard. We saw that a large wooden altar had been erected at one end, with a ten-by-ten-foot Japanese flag for a background. The red-dot flag always infuriated us. We called it the inflamed rectum and other nice names. That morning, with such thoughts in our minds, we were spaced over the cinders as if for calisthenics. An interpreter told us that this was to be a ceremony and instructed us what to do. First, Lieutenant Yamada stood before the altar and swiftly recited a speech praising the Emperor, informing the god-ruler in absentia that he, Hirohito, was being honored even by the lowly foreign prisoners. Finished with that, with a flourish he drew his sword and pointed it toward Tokyo. We prisoners, according to instructions, all raised our arms and when Yamada began shouting "*Banzai*" we shouted too. But I yelled other words, which are better left to the imagination. The interpreters could not catch them because of the roar of voices. That ended the ceremony and never again was I called upon to hail the Emperor.

Time for Diesel Bluff

When the new year started I was taken from the gasoline drum factory and assigned to the big machine shop, now supplied with men and ready for production. Eight other Americans including Sergeant Minor were to be tried out. This was the test — was I or was I not a diesel engineer?

An interpreter showed us over the big place. Some of the machinery was from America, antiquated by fifty years, discarded by American manufacturers. Some of it was fair stuff, made in Japan. We were asked if we could operate machines. That was the tip-off that we did not really need to be diesel engineers. Sergeant Minor chirped that he could run a drill press. Surrounded by strange machinery that fairly leered at me, I picked on something that might, just might, be easy and told them that I was an experienced man on the file bench.

Immediately I was introduced to a man named Suzuki, but we did not shake hands. I did tell him, though, that I understood a little of his language and would rather work here than in the drum shop. He was the foreman. I was to be with him for a long time.

This Suzuki was an uneducated man and crude in many ways, but he had a sense of humor and was the only Nip I ever met who really knew anything about mechanics or the making of things with his hands. He was proud to vanity of his craftsmanship. That morning he forgot all about the other Yanks, who could not speak his tongue, and concentrated on showing me delicate tools and engine parts which he had made. Considering the rough tools and materials with which he had to work, his stuff was good and I told him so. From that day on I was Suzuki's pet.

They gave us handful of Americans tests on the file benches and machines. Only four of us were selected to remain on what was called the *kikai** work detail. Minor was one of the four.

Showman for Japs

The test that the Jap technicians gave me was a sham and a fraud. They did not even look at my filed pieces. They would have passed me had my stuff fallen under requirements, which they may have done. Because I was an American who spoke some of their language they wanted me so that they could hear about my country twelve thousand miles away. They wished to hear about the war in the Philippines and a hundred and one other things of interest to these humble, unlettered workers in dark Japan. Were they going to let me go? No, indeed! So I put on a good show for them.

Looking back at it, it seems to me that I must have spent most of my time those first few months on the Kikai detail just sitting around entertaining the Japs with stories of America, and this and that. I worked in a hint occasionally that I was not getting enough to eat at the barrack mess. They didn't have much either but now and then they gave me a crumb.

At first no Nip gave me any specific duty, but each day I filed a few pieces for a one-striper named Sumitami and afterward would sit by the fire resting my weary bones until time to return to prison. I always had a group of work dodgers to talk to. Nobody appeared to care about the loafing if the bosses weren't around.

January 24 came along and I had a birthday but no cake.

Meet the Koreans

I began to notice silent Orientals at the fringe of the groups around the fires. They appeared to pay about as little attention as deaf persons would, but when no Nips were observing they would give me smiles or

*Machine shop.

nods of puzzling friendliness. All at once it snapped home to me that they were not Japs but Koreans. Some of these people had been brought to Japan under sham contracts to work for Japan during the war. In time the Japs quit the sham and merely brought the Koreans to the home islands in herds as virtual slaves. Some of these were in that category. After my return to the States, I read in a newspaper that Koreans had done considerable intelligence work for the Allies.

The Koreans, I learned, were watched and treated almost like prisoners except that they were not all locked up at night. They weren't supposed, however, to be on the streets; they were handled much like Negro slaves in the earlier days of the American South. These big-boned boys often could not speak Japanese as well as I could, and there was an element of humor in an American slave and a Korean slave holding converse in the tongue of our captors.

Physically these people reminded me of the Pueblo Indians of New Mexico. Although they were yellow, slant-eyed Orientals and in a few rare cases were intermarried with the Japs, I found them to be liberal and kindly. Only a few swallowed the Japanese propaganda. Most of them were sympathetic with us Americans. I soon learned that they made loyal and dependable friends; so I selected a few as my allies in pulling the wool over Jap eyes.

About one out of every five of the Koreans had at some time been exposed to the Christian religion by American missionaries in their home land. They had a good opinion of America but could not realize the greatness of our country because of their illiterate and, as a whole, unenlightened lives. They had thought at the beginning of the war that Japan would make slaves of all America and rule it as Korea was dominated. I began to reeducate them. At first it was difficult to make them comprehend that the Japs did not have a chance of crossing the Rockies and marching on Washington. For one reason I wasn't certain enough myself, in early 1943, that the Japs couldn't do it, so I wasn't very convincing. I had no military dope to know what Uncle Sam was doing, though I did not suppose the American people were taking the war lying down. But when our forces began to stop the Japs in the Pacific, a change of thinking began to dawn among the sturdy fellows. I told them that Uncle Samuel and the Allies, including my country of Texas, were going to polish off the Germans first, then back the Japs off their own islands. The boys from Korea would grin at that and all but prayed with us for the great day to arrive.

Although no single Korean slave can be given credit for directly saving me from starvation, disease and a grave — or box of ashes — in Japan, the combined effort of the group did help me when other Americans were hungry. During the war years Japan never had a real abundance of food. From the first everything was rationed. Japanese born after the start of the war with China often had never seen chewing gum or tasted ice cream or other dairy products. Chocolate and coffee were some sort of nonexistent delicacies which their older relatives talked about — they were in a class with the samurai, feudal barons and castles. But the Koreans were not stingy with what tiny pinches of knick-knacks they could get. *They* didn't hoard.

The Wonder of Plenty

I got a great kick out of telling the kids how we in America could buy all the gumdrops and sweet drinks we desired for only a small part of our daily wages. They never really believed it, but the stories were as interesting to them as fairy tales. One may wonder how I got in touch with children. In the land of the rising sun, the youngsters of some working classes never attended school. They enter shops and factories as apprentices and become the lower-paid semi-skilled people. Some of these were in the Yodogawa Works.

Equally the older people were incredulous when told Americans could buy every kind of meat at the stores. They had no conception of a meat market. In Japan a person gets beef only if he is a member of the privileged classes or makes special arrangements when an animal is butchered in his neighborhood. During the war even their steady fish diet was short. For civilians there weren't any canned goods at all. Most of the farmlands were given over to rice. The tiny gardens, crowded in everywhere, produced mostly cabbage, squash, cucumbers, and a vegetable called daikon, which is apparently a cross between a turnip and a white radish. The daikon was long, white and starchy and was boiled in soup, pickled, fried in fish oil when such was obtainable, and sometimeswas dried and ground and used as flour. It did not appeal to the American taste.

Alfalfa Soup

Prisoners got very few of these vegetables except by theft. The so-called soup was often made of the dried daikon tops. Once we stole a bale of alfalfa hay and made more tasty soup from it. The Japs flavor their cooking with either soybean sauce or a paste made from fermented beans and wheat and called miso. It is just about the only flavor agreeable to Americans. No Jap I ever asked knew what vanilla was; so I suppose it is not used in Japan.

We prisoners realized from the first that the Nips weren't up to snuff on cooking and were convinced when we saw them waste the few spoonfuls of sugar they were allowed monthly by using it with bean sauce and a large, coarse saltwater fish. The concoction tasted about like what I imagine a strawberry sundae would turn out to be with Limburger cheese and garlic.

Strange Use for Garlic

Our conviction was that compared to Americans, Europeans and Chinese, the Japs did not know how to cook or eat. I would admire their cuisine more if they used garlic, chili pepper or some other high seasoning to an excess. Garlic isn't used in cooking. It is sold on the market for pregnant women or to those who wish to keep the men away. The Japanese — lower classes anyhow — don't even put salt in their pasty boiled rice. Sometimes they have flour, usually of old rice, but appear to do little baking. Before the war, I learned, there were a few commercial bakeries in the cities where those who had acquired a taste for white bread could buy it.

Ate the Gods' Food

In the homes the women mix the rice flour with water and make steamed dough balls called mochi. This is used at the New Year as symbolic food for the gods. On that day every family is supposed to place mochi balls in their homes, or at shrines, in order to have good luck through the year and keep evil spirits away. Sometimes it is attached to bicycles or automobiles to prevent accidents or a tire blowing out. Flour was so scarce in Japan at the 1945 New Year that the Nips had to substitute mochis made of light clay for the gods, and themselves eat the real mochis.

The national strong drink in Japan, sake, is brewed from rice. What I saw had a pale sherry color and an acid taste. There are several varieties. The one called shiro is white and is the poorest grade, being the dregs of the vats. It smelled like yeast with vinegar. A sweet sake was called marin. No sake was ever issued to prisoners, but occasionally a man would steal a bottle, taste it, screw up his face, bribe a guard or trade it for black market food. Japs would get drunk on it sometimes. Several alcoholic old army hands claimed they were cured of drinking by the stuff.

Grasshoppers Are Tasty

Queasiness hit my stomach when I first saw Japs eating toasted grasshoppers. Daring to try one, I found it tasted much like potato chips and I acquired a liking for them. A starving prisoner will eat anything, almost. There was one food we balked at, however. It was a stinking and revolting mess made of green moss and seaweed from the bottoms of the canals, decaying vegetable matter tasting like what my imagination tells me refuse from the floor of a fish market might be. The Japs liked it.

Dogs are supposed to be somewhat sacred in Japan, but an empty belly forgets its reverence sometimes. I have seen Japanese bicker and dicker over a poor little pooch caught alone in the streets. Dog meat demanded a premium when our navy blockaded the home islands and made offshore fishing a precarious occupation. Horse meat was a delicacy but the practical Nips hesitated to kill a horse, what with the shortage of other motive power and transportation.

There was one other food that I ate without revolting: silkworms. They came crushed and molded into balls. I supposed — without knowing — that they were the worms taken from the cocoons before they had time to gnaw their way out and ruin the fiber. Fortunately silkworm cakes were tasteless.

We Eat American Fertilizer

In the States ground bones and fish scraps are often used for fertilizer. In Japan it is called *sakana ko** and eaten with relish. As a prisoner I once stole a bag of the stuff, and my friends and I supplemented our rice diet with it. It was genuine imported stuff from America, too. To prove it, the bag bore the maker's name (based in Los Angeles, California, U.S.A.) and the warning, "To be used for fertilizer, not fit for human consumption."

We often discussed the subject of how welcome a can of U.S. dog food would be to us, and surmised that our pet pooches at home were faring better than we were. Chickens and eggs were known in Japan, but were unknown to us. They were strictly on the national ration list and we didn't have the stamps. Neither did the coolie earning three dollars a day, with eggs at ten dollars each.

Soybeans were used as a rice substitute by the coolies. Prisoners rarely received the beans in my camp, although sometimes we could steal them. The Japs mixed the hard little beans with their rice before cooking. Rice boils quickly, beans slowly. Such a mixture had hard little kernels in it. The coolies grumbled because the uncooked beans made wind in their stomachs and they wished the government would do something about it. Prisoners sometimes got bean pulp made by rolling and crushing all the oil from the bean.

I have dwelt at length on food. So did our bellies. Men with stomach disorders, malaria, dysentery, were compelled to eat what American dogs would lift a lip at. If they rebelled — well, for a starving man to miss three meals might mean death. One boy, on the sissy side, went weakly amok and shrilled, "My mother wouldn't want me to eat this nasty Jap stuff, and I won't do it." He missed two meals and died.

But by and large we all became members of the Unwilling Association of Rice Eaters.

Sergeant Thinks Up Torture

In the late winter of 1942–43 it was a nightmare for me to leave the shop and return to the barrack. One reason was that after fifty men

*Powdered fish.

or so had died out of our four hundred, the Japs decided we needed more physical toughening to reduce the mortality rate. After evening *tenko* the men were ordered to strip to the waist and rub themselves with small straw brushes that were furnished us. "Rub chest and arms with honorable vigor" was the order. If a man held his thumb between brush and body it was found out when the guards inspected to see if our skins were ruddy. The penalty for faking was to be rubbed by the guards until the skin was bleeding. Or if their mania for mass punishment was uppermost, they would order all hands outside to the cinders and make us use the brushes with more honorable vigor than ever, then give us quick marching time in place until the weakest men dropped. After that they would let us go with a few nighty-night kicks.

This stupid punishment may have contributed to the hardening of some men, but for the most part it only weakened us. We were all sick men suffering from a variety of diseases and that one great pain which is worse than all others — starvation. Hunger for a few days does not hurt a person, but slow starvation is another story. Prolonged periods of depriving the body from the essential nutritive foods weakens it in all parts. After a time the body is no longer maintained at a normal temperature. The pains of slow starvation are more maddening than those of a wound, fever, hard work, tropical sun, or fatigue.

This scrub-brush torture was the master idea of the most hated and infamous character in the Jap army personnel in charge of us. He was Sergeant Akumatsu, and he must have been working for promotion to the position of Satan in Hell. As the mildest of our epithets we called him the Beast. Commonplace but descriptive. He was as large as the average American, and that he had a powerful right arm I learned early in the game. He was the only Jap guard I ever met who could come any way near knocking me off my feet while I faced him, braced at attention. The Beast was really more animal than man. He would lurk in concealment like a panther on a tree to catch a prisoner disobeying one of the hundreds of rules he set down for us.

Only a Broken Nose

Akumatsu caught me stepping out of line to avoid a mud puddle as I was being conducted to work. He came snarling like a crazy dog, yelling "*Kioske da*," which was the order for me to face him at attention. How many times he hit my face with his fist and open hand I do not know, because after my nose was crushed and spouting blood, and my eyes were blind from clouts and tears, I wasn't counting anymore but praying that somehow I would get a chance to choke him to death with my bare hands. I was lucky to get off with only a broken nose. The Beast broke my nose more than once before I left Japan, which made it heal crooked. Army surgeons broke it once more for me after I was liberated and performed a wonderful job of straightening it. Persons who knew me before the war say I have a better-looking nose now than before.

When the typical Jap guard tried to slap me it was sometimes more humorous than offensive. They had to tiptoe to reach me and I would laugh. That would make them furious, but they couldn't add a cubit to their height and do any better; so they would quit in disgust.

Had there not been other American faces that the Beast wished to pound that morning I probably would have been beaten to the ground and gotten a few ribs kicked in. But someone must have doubled a fist, or snarled, or laughed grimly, for suddenly the Beast left me and attacked elsewhere; his throat sounds were worse than a hyena's.

Electric Feet

In our barrack at night we ordinarily had about an hour after tenko until lights out. When chill blackness fell over us, we had to be on our shelves sleeping, or pretending to be. For me it was often pretense. Those nights were a bedlam of pain-cries, coughing, psychopathic storms, what-not. I don't know who suffered most, but the men with swelling, spitting, rotting feet from beri-beri cried out the most. There was no such thing as aspirin to quiet them. Some of the "electric feet" burned so that the men soaked them in icy water to alleviate the agony. This wasn't good. It seemed to result in a lot of toe amputations.

One cold morning when a buddy got up, he shook a couple of his own toes out of his blankets. They had come off in the night.

I suffered so much from beri-beri that I could not get in more than one good night's sleep a week, in the early prison months. I just walked the floor in the dark, bumping into other men doing the same thing, until exhaustion forced me back to the sleeping shelf.

Men who were able to get downstairs into the tin- or metal-working shop could get hot baths from a plating vat of fairly clean water. Not in the vat; we would douse pails of water over ourselves. I took the bath as much to get warm as to cleanse myself. It was hazardous for any of us to go down and bathe, because we had to go stark naked down the outside stairs in the cold and return with steaming bodies. The shop people did not want our possibly infected clothing in the shop. They were pneumonia trips, those quick flittings down and back.

Sick men could not take the baths at all. Our three or four prisoner medical attendants could not get around often to bathing the patients. Everybody had body lice. Even when we bathed, we could not get rid of them because they remained in our clothing. Eventually I had plenty of opportunity to keep my garments lice-free by boiling them in the shop. Some men who were not kept awake by pain would be by the lice. I have seen them standing at the windows at night picking the bugs off. Many men had to sleep in their clothing because of insufficient covering. I had managed to keep a couple of scraps of dirty canvas from Philippine days and they helped a lot.

Prisoners from Everywhere

A more mixed group of three or four hundred men could scarcely have been found than those in our barrack. No wonder they were tormented by emotional conflicts, by racial idiosyncrasies, psychopathic blowups. A year or two later, helping briefly with the typing of names in the Yodogawa office, I discovered that thirty-two states of the Union were represented by the prisoners. There were American Indians, two or three Mexicans, and men of racial descent from every country in Europe except Russia. Of the Allies, we had only no Chinese and Russians. Many professional soldiers and sailors were included. The average age was around thirty years. Many younger men pulled the average down heavily. There were men beyond forty. Many degrees of intelligence, education and tempers were represented. We were a hodgepodge of humanity, friendships, cliques, and dislikes, the hate of captivity being the chief tie that bound us.

There was often bickering and quarreling, and some fighting. Perhaps the most memorable battle occurred something like midway through our captivity. It started between a sergeant and a K.P. I was right at hand and stepped between them, got them apart. But catcalls went up all over the room, meant for me, and advice:

"Keep y'r nose out of it, Mac." Such shouts as, "Let the bastards kill one another. They're no-good sons of bitches anyhow. Who sent f'r you, Mac? Back off."

Well, I didn't like either one of the men. They were despicable. I listened to the profane shouting and backed off. The pair went to it. Other men joined in. The yelling, cheering, the thud of fists on flesh and bones, the cries of frightened psychopaths, of the sick, all was punctuated by the crushing of benches, the splitting of boards and timbres. It ended up with panting men, bloody faces, loose teeth, and broken-down shelves. Oh, it was a sight, that room, by the time guards arrived.

In the investigation it came out that I could have stopped the affair at its beginning. I was slapped freely for not doing so.

Sleep between Corpses

As I paced the floor with burning feet, in the early months, there was often a corpse on the bench in the center hallway waiting to be burned the next day. We pacing men would chase nibbling rats away from the bodies. Major Reardon, our American commanding officer, had to go daily as a witness to watch the dead being reduced to ashes. As the corpses were carried out of the room we prisoners would stand at attention and salute. To the Nips it was just another report that one more captive had died "due to natural causes."

Almost every morning one would hear such exclamations. "Well, I'll be damned, Old Chief cashed his chips last night. One of the strongest too. You never can tell." And we couldn't. Apparently healthy men would die and skeletons would survive. And further morning talk might be, "Hendrick and Joe'll kick in before noon. Don't know how Smith hangs on." One morning I awoke with a dead man on each side of me, snuggled close as if they had been trying to get warm.

So many men died that winter that it became a topic of conversation among the Japanese civilian factory workers. They offered little help or sympathy because their regulations forbade it. They didn't care much either, for we were just foreigners and prisoners.

No Smiling Faces

It was a cheerless world there in Yodogawa that first winter. I tried to shut out some of the horror by keeping my thoughts from my sur-roundings and dreaming of things in America like a warm fire and nearby delicatessen. I would have gone insane had I dwelt on the miseries. At first we were not permitted to look out the windows over the street. The other windows showed only dirty canals, black factory buildings and slums. There were no trees, no grass, no birds, but I held on doggedly and often thought of the lines:

> Two men look out through the same bars;
> One sees the mud and one sees the stars.

When we were allowed, finally, to stand at the forbidden windows and look at the open sea, many native people passed on the street below but I never saw a smiling face.

I have been asked how some of us kept our morale so high and our mental equipment functioning normally. We didn't act as normal human individuals. All of us were dominated by physical and mental fears. The minds and nerve of many men were broken completely. We who were strong carried the burdens of those weaker than us. Although all of us were in the same situation, it was proven that a society which governs all with a general set of rules does not provide sufficiently for differences in individuals.

Mild Sabotage

In the machine shop the Japs treated me civilly because the No. 1 technician, Suzuki, told them that I was his slave, and thus I gained great face. None of them dared strike me or urge me too much about working. A lot of the time Suzuki wasn't around to keep an eye on me. At such times I would loaf at the fire and rest my beri-beri feet and tell stories. Sometimes I could translate an American dirty joke sufficiently to get a laugh from my associates. I often made comparisons between Japan and America, without credit to the flowery kingdom. I'd get angry and curse. The Nips would laugh like idiots at my spleen.

It was lucky for me that these people were not too ethical or patriotic in their country's war effort, for it enabled me to make suggestions about not working when the boss wasn't around, or do other things which fell naturally to them about slowing up work. It was planned sabotage, of course.

This class of people just could not think for themselves, outside their small daily duties which were patterned for them. The Japanese life and character is so conditioned by a culture that is hundreds of years old that they do not have to do any extensive thinking. I learned this after observing them for only a few weeks. Ruth Benedict, American anthropologist, explains this factor in her analysis of Japanese character in a recent book.[1] The Japanese factory workers had nothing that we would call education. They never forgot, though, that I was a mere American prisoner, and when they had read bad news, or had it read to them — propaganda stuff about the cruel Americans brutally slaying thousands of their fellow countrymen — they would come in of mornings with ugly stares at me. But like the simple folk they were they would soon forget that and ask me if such things were true. Thus I would hear the news. Also they liked to see my reactions to such insults as "brutal Yanks!"

After months with these people they grew to trust me and perhaps to like me. The same was true of Sergeant Minor. The sergeant and I were together there until the spring of 1945. He and I were not watched as closely as other prisoners because of the human element involved in guarding us. The Japanese Army wasn't afraid of two men doing any great harm by being left alone in the factory full of other supposedly patriotic Nipponese. As civilian watchman, Minor and I had a short little Jap named Oni whom we called "Gunga Din" because he looked like the movie version of that character from Kipling's story. Gunga Din was a thief among thieves, because of the fact that he was paid a very low salary. He often told Minor and me to steal something from a factory warehouse while he kept watch for army guards. We followed his orders with a grin because we were always given half of whatever we stole for him. This we could in turn trade on the black market for food. Gunga

Din was probably the lowest-salaried and most likeable adult Nip in our factory. He was acquainted with everyone from the top official down to the man who dipped the sewage from the disposal vats.

Thieves for Black Market

At first Minor and I gave little thought to sabotage. We were concerned almost altogether with preserving our health and obtaining extra food and medicines. We enlisted men drew ten *sen* a day as pay — about a cent in U.S. money — but were not permitted to spend it, as the Japs did not want us buying and using more food than we were issued. Officers drew forty yen a month and would pass some of it to Minor and me to contact the black market. At first the Nips were reluctant to listen to our appeals, saying they would be beaten if caught, which was true. We convinced them, though, that rules were made to be broken and if they expected us to work for them they must bring us food to give us strength. So eventually we got a supply line to work.

As my agents I picked a couple of old Nips whom I had caught stealing brass from the foundry warehouse and burying it by a hole in the fence through which they could reach at night and move the stuff out to the black market. I hinted that if they did not play ball with me I would report them to Gold Striper Suzuki. They grinned at me, knowing that I wouldn't, the cunning monkeys! But I had made a correct guess as to their characters, so daily these men managed to slip me the nod as indication that they had stuff hidden, in the washroom or behind a steel pile. I attended to these matters mostly while Minor covered in the shop for me, but not always by any means. The sergeant was a master hand himself at hooking fish.

Guards Grow Suspicious

For the most part, we tried to get vitamin tablets and medicine to treat our beri-beri. The food brought in was usually fish and dried vegetables. Before we built up a working fund the cagey old men would let us have only half the stuff they brought. We would have to smuggle that into the barrack in our clothing, distribute it to the officers and sick friends, and collect. Then we would go back and get the rest. But we managed in time to build up an available fund and take everything at once.

The guards began to grow suspicious. It got so that we had to eat all the food ourselves because it was too bulky to take in and could only sneak in medicines. Thus we bought less food and more pills. We ate the food because it was too precious to take a chance of a guard's getting it. Besides, we would have received a beating.

Once I was caught taking in medicine and had to stand three hours with a bucket of water on my head and holding a bamboo pole on my outstretched arms. It was cold weather. I wasn't strong. I fell. The water spilled over me. I was soaked. The guard beat me for clumsiness and made me stand again. I lasted three hours only because the guard wasn't always in sight and I would set the bucket down and lean on the pole.

Shoe Racket Is Discovered

In the domain of the Heavenly Emperor, leather shoes are scarce even in peacetime. During the war it was all but impossible for Jap civilians to buy a pair as good as the American army shoe. Most of us prisoners had been allowed to keep the shoes we wore at capture. It was still cold spring weather when all prisoners were taken from their work to the cinder yard one evening earlier than usual. We gabbled eagerly that it was to be another distribution of Red Cross boxes. Others were certain we were to be moved to a better prison. I thought we were going to catch hell, and we did.

The snarling face of our commander, Sergeant Hirose, had tipped me off. He barked for us to undress, shoes and all, no sick man or anybody else excepted. Our clothing, in piles before our naked legs, was searched to the last seam. Men in whose rags money was found had to step out and prove where they got it. As we stood nude and shivering the interpreter mounted a table along with the fiery Hirose, who drew his sword and whacked the air. They spouted words like this:

"The Japanese military police have found that some prisoners have been selling American shoes to civilians. That is not good because it reduces your ability to work. Whoever has sold shoes must step forward and confess. It is the shoes of the sickest men, who cannot be here, that have been sold. If you confess you will save the group from mass punishment."

They waited with cunning patience while we shivered. When fifteen minutes had passed and no man had opened a stubborn mouth we were ordered to attention and any man who moved an eyelash was slapped. Factory officials and town civilians came up to see the fun. The guards paraded us in a circle. Nobody confessed. The guards became impatient. Sergeant Hirose gave another order.

The Prayer Punishment

The order was to take a position that was sometimes called "saying our prayers." It was to kneel on the sharp cinders and set the weight of our bodies back on our feet, our toes taking most of the torture on the cinders. When we were all in this position the guards passed down the line whacking each man on the head with a long hammer handle, a sword, or a bamboo pole.

Evidently I looked extra guilty or had a hateful expression, for a guard named Niasta whacked me until tears rolled down my cheeks. When no confession was forthcoming the interpreter began walking back and forth repeating. "You must make honest confession. Are many guilties." From that day on we named the fellow Many Guilties.

Four hours of torture went by and still nobody confessed. Men who tried to shift position or rub circulation into their feet were whacked. Darkness was coming on and the Nips were getting hungry and sore, whereupon they thought of a new wrinkle. They dragged or carried all the patients from the so-called hospital room in the barrack and made them kneel with us. These men were suffering from everything in the book — fever, beri-beri, tuberculosis, pneumonia. The interpreter told us these men would be stripped too if somebody didn't confess very quick.

One Man Finally Cracks

The situation was that more than fifty pairs of shoes had been sold. They brought good prices on the sneak market and put lots of rice into empty bellies. Each man who had been selling shoes felt certain that the police had found out about other deals than his. So they kept mum, just hoping, for by now Hirose had informed us that the guilties would be shot.

Despite the treat, a man who could no longer stand the sight of the suffering sick spoke up. He was probably the least guilty and offensive of them all, for he had disposed of but one pair of shoes. I consider him a real hero. We expected to see him shot forthwith, but the Nips only began beating him, ordering him to tell the names of others. He wouldn't do that but when he was practically insensible they got from him the name of the man to whom he had sold. It was one of our shop Koreans, about the best friend of Minor and I had among that race.

The Korean was brought. They laid fists, swords and clubs on him till all his front teeth were spit out on the ground and he lay bleeding and with torn clothes. The interpreter kept whining, "Still many guilties. Perhaps somebody else know. You confess now you not be shot." Men couldn't take it forever. Another, then another, spoke up. Some spilled the beans on others. The innocent men were then allowed to return to the barrack, for the Japs were tired. But the investigation was carried on throughout the night, with some men remaining on the cinders holding poles under their ankles.

The next day several Jap civilians were brought in and about two dozen pairs of shoes were recovered. From that day on every prisoner who still owned shoes had to register them and label them with his name. We were threatened with death if another pair was sold. I slept with my shoes after that. The Japs listed every man involved in the shoe business as a dangerous character.

The Gangster Questionnaires

As time went on the Nips thought of something else — questionnaires. It was a trick to drag information out of us. One of the queries was, Have you ever been a gangster in Chicago? Two careful old sergeants of the regular army meekly wrote that they had not been exactly gangsters, but that they had done some bootlegging. That answer really puckered the brows of the Nips.

We were periodically given papers to be filled out. Officers and men above the average of intelligence were asked to write essays on such subjects as "Who I think will win the war and why," "My impression of Japan," "What I think of the Japanese army," "Production and distribution of food in wartime Japan." They hoped of course that some men would write valuable military information or make suggestions which could be put to use. The bribe for the best paper was a box of tea or an extra bowl of rice.

I wrote an essay comparing the Japanese army to the bandit troops of Pancho Villa in Mexico thirty years before, being careful to tell nothing about our own forces. Oddly enough, we were never punished for these frank and contemptuous expressions. I think that was because such papers went to high headquarters and were not read locally.

One set of questionnaires had very harmless questions with a punchy one inserted now and then, such as "How long did it take you to travel from San Francisco to Manila before the war started?" Or, "What kind of a boat did you travel on?" The replies we gave to these would have made a dog grin. One man wrote, "In a birch-bark canoe, the chief means of water transportation in the U.S." Other questions were "What is your favorite movie?" "Favorite food?" "What is your hobby?" To that last one I replied, "Ropin' goats," and went through a terrific sweat trying to make it clear to the examiner what I meant.

Change of Guards

By warm weather in 1943, at least 250 of our men had died and 100 more were just short of the exit. None of us were fat and healthy. Thirty of the worst cases were moved to a joke hospital under a concrete stadium in a section of Osaka across the Yodo River from us. Word came back that they had no fire and were given only one-third rations because they were suffering from maladies which prevented them from working. My friend Corporal Clinton Metzler was one of the prisoners sent there. After liberation an American newspaper described his conditions in the prison[2]:

> Metzler stuck it out gamely at Yodogawa, working long hours in a steel mill, where wearing of shoes was prohibited. Early in 1943 he got "hot" or

"electric" feet, caused from a protein deficiency and lack of foot covering. Other men had lost parts of their feet.

Finally, when the A-10 patient was unable to work any longer he was sent to a hospital. "The doctors there did hardly anything, while my feet got worse and gangrene set in," Metzler explained. "The skin just peeled off from my toes, and the bones became so soft that a doctor was able to cut them off with finger-nail clippers."

About this time our army guards were replaced with civilians hired by the factory. Presumably all soldiers were needed at the front. However, we were not completely abandoned by the army. Sergeant Hirose, the commander, remained with his stooges, the Beast, Niasata and Ito. They had charge of the food supplies, which were furnished partly by the military and partly by the Yodogawa works. It was common knowledge that the four noncoms were selling a lot of our food outside, but what could we do about it?

The civilian guards were men physically and mentally unfit for military service. When we and they were lined up for introductions I was incredulous. They had the mugs of monkeys, morons, clowns. A living comic strip.

We hoped for better treatment from them than from the soldiers and got worse. It was tougher to be slapped by the pop-eyed, bucktoothed weaklings than by a big soldier. They wore misfit, slouchy army uniforms without insignia. They would lean a shoulder against a wall, with hands in pockets, cigarette dangling from loose lips, and look important. Their prisoner-dusters were axe handles. They would yell for us to salute them, but never return the salute. They would punish us for the lack of a button on our rotting garments, often as not with their own collar or cuff unbuttoned.

I figured they were some sort of political appointees.

Nobody Liked 'Em

These civilian police were called *kabihe** (kay-bee-hay)—and Yanks and Jap factory people hated them from the first. The hard-working Nips regarded them as loafers. The kabihe drew the same pay and food and

---

*Home guard soldiers.

clothing allowances. They turned the Nips to thinking more of us prisoners. They would rather back us up than the kabihe.

Suzuki, my boss, and all the office personnel in the shop with Minor and me disliked the spying guards so much that Mino and I were not discouraged in outwitting them. When they appeared in the shop on inspection trips the Nips would deliberately halt work and glare at them. The apprentice kids would make catcalls or furtively throw a bolt. The spies would sputter helplessly. They tried to catch Minor and me in idleness, but practically always when they entered we would be industriously at our machines, though five minutes before we might have been yarning with a gang of listeners.

Still Suzuki's Pets

Suzuki would brag to visiting foremen from other factories in the area that Minor and I were the best American prisoners in Japan. There was some vanity in this; he liked to shine in every aspect. He would laughingly tell us before the visitors that in a few more months our hair would turn black and our eyes grow slanted and we would be Japanese. He recommended the eating of "*takusan*"* rice to hurry the process.

Suzuki knew that Minor and I broke many regulations, but he kept silent and looked the other way. For example, he was well aware that prisoners were not supposed to get war news, but he also knew that we were managing to do so right along. He liked to discuss the war with us and hear our opinions of events. We were probably the most educated men he had ever talked with.

The boss's favoritism — we could loaf by the day under his nose and never hear a reprimand — gave us more and more face with the others as the months went by. Through the resulting favorable connections we were able to beg, steal and bargain more freely, so that with more food we began to be halfway healthy and gain some weight; and the beri-beri eased somewhat.

In a way Suzuki was repaid for his kindness to us. We instructed ignorant workers. The semi-skilled men were being continually pulled off the

*Much.

job for army service. They were replaced with slaves from the hill country of Korea. Minor and I became highly valuable as instructors and workmen and whatnot. The office and supply department were careless and got to depending more and more on us to keep track of new parts, their number and where they were stored. We were given personal lockers in which to keep our few clothes and old scraps of stuff that prisoners accumulate.

Emery Dust Sabotage

These special privileges did not remove our dislike of captivity. We could never forget that we were slaves. Nor did we forget that we were American soldiers. Disgusted at being told to stick our hands into grease and smear engine pistons and the insides of cylinders before shipping them out to be assembled in marine diesel motors, we would dab our grease-coated hands into emery dust at the grinding wheels and work the destructive stuff on to the smooth surfaces. The finer dust would not be noticed and within a few days motors would be returned for repairs. We could see how nicely the emery had cut the cylinders and Minor would smile his slow and gentle smile.

A few anti-aircraft gun parts were turned into our shop. We were not supposed to know what they were or to work on them. Often a Jap wanting to leave his lathe for a cup of tea would ask Minor or me to watch while he was gone. One day I got to a lathe where cylinders for flak gun equilibrators were being bored out. I set the bit deep and bored the solid metal end of the tube down to paper thinness. I was able to accomplish this repeatedly thereafter.

When those pieces were returned with the ends broken out, probably at the first test firing, the Nips were puzzled. Foundry technicians were called in, and they howled that the metal wasn't properly tempered. The next set of tubes were tempered too brittle for the handmade bits to bite into. They broke the teeth of machines. The shop foreman became disgusted with the foundry and decided to temper the metal in the shop. They laid the batch of tubes in the yard, piled straw on top, and lit a match. When the metal cooled slowly it was soft enough to work but also was weakened so that it couldn't stand the strain of the recoil. So another batch was spoiled.

Sabotage by Proxy

Often Minor and I did not have to touch a machine to cause destruction. We just stood back and refrained from giving advice while the half-trained workers destroyed their own materials. Strictly following the laws of our country, I could be prosecuted for revealing that Allied prisoners of war participated in any sabotage activities whatsoever. General Wainwright reported such activities at the prison camp where he interned in Manchuria, and as a free American citizen now I am taking the same privilege.[3]

One trick of ours resulted from Japan's having been so densely populated for many hundreds of years that wood fuel was scarce, all but unobtainable. The shop had wooden molds for making motor parts. We were afraid to risk burning these on cold mornings, but the Nips could get as cold as we, so we remarked to a bunch of apprentice boys that these molds would sure make a nice fire. The kids didn't know any better than to fall for the suggestion. By springtime every mold in the storeroom had been burned.

Because Korean slaves and even Nips themselves were stealing and selling steel drill bits, Minor was ordered to take charge of the bits and keep them under lock and key. Bits were often broken because of uncertain tempering. Minor found some old, broken bits under a dusty shelf. He sharpened them and put them in place of good bits and sent out the good ones by Korean friends to be sold on the greedy black market. That put more food in our stomachs.

When Jap apprentices asked Minor to check out a drill of a certain size, he would give a drill a tiny bit larger. As the piece passed down the production line each operator would get a larger drill. Since speed and production, in Japan as in America, is the demand of war, these borings were rarely checked. When the machinery was bolted together the holes were a few thousandths of an inch too large and the stuff could not stand up long under strain and vibration.

Splash Goes the Yen

Essentially, Japan and the Yodogawa works were betting the Yank prisoners would make them a profit. Minor and I lost them that bet at

Yodogawa, simply by throwing materials away. We tossed so much stuff through the windows into a canal that by the end of the war we must have concealed thousands of dollars' worth.

One day when food was short and Minor and I were sweating and grumbling, carrying oilers across a narrow footbridge to a warehouse, he paused and said, "Hell, I'm tired of working for these slant-eyed heathen. For two sen I'd drop this thing into the water." "I'll pay you the two sen," I said. And he dropped the oiler, ker-splash!

Now, these oilers were expensive, worth probably five thousand yen. They were compression boxes with tubes running out to lubricate the bearings of diesel engines. They were not, they could not be, made in Japan. These had been confiscated in the Philippines and French Indochina. We knew the careless Nips would never be able to check on us, nor suspect us. We were just dumb prisoners. So we dropped thirty of the boxes into the canal that afternoon.

The aftermath was interesting. When the shortage of oilers was discovered they tried to check invoices but could not find where guilt lay. We heard several telephone calls by gold stripers trying frantically to locate the essential parts. For a while some work stopped because they could not be found.

Admittedly it was the lowest sort of treachery against Suzuki, but we were Americans doing the best we could for our war. Our captors were not living up to their obligations in housing and feeding us. We were not even assured of living from day to day. We had to do something to let off steam and amuse ourselves. If it counted, so much the better.

Food Stealing Is Thrilling

With the cherry-blossom season at hand — though there were no blossoms in the dirty world where we served our masters — all but ten of our officers were sent away to another prison, on Sikoku Island.* The Nips wished them to leave believing that things were going to be better for us; so each of us was given half a tiny watermelon on the day of departure, and a little extra rice.

*One of the four main islands of the Japanese Empire.

However, our food supply was dragging. More men died of nothing but malnutrition. There should be some answer as to why some men died and some lived. Mostly the ones who survived had access to outside sources for food, such as I had. That may be the answer in part. Men not in a position to raid the black market were becoming desperate. I saw Americans snatch up discarded scraps of vegetables and fish heads from refuse heaps. These they had to wash and boil and eat secretly.

The warm weather made us more active. Wholesale stealing of food set in. Stealing was highly punishable. Our kebihe guards became more watchful and cunning, and in counteraction we became sharper to outwit them.

Minor and I had to become more alert. We took advantage of our freedom to wander around the big factory area under pretense of going after machine parts. We would carry a sack with bolts in it. The guards watched from the high fence. There was a factory cafeteria behind which food was stored in a warehouse. Sometimes after trucks were unloaded the stuff would lie outside for a while. We would lurk behind convenient steel piles or a corner until the guards were out of sight, then snatch a box of fish or a bundle of vegetables. We'd dump the bolts out of the sack, put the food in, and hurry and sweat getting the bolts back on top. If the sack were looked into, only bolts were to be seen. In this act we were coolies, carrying the bag on the typical Japanese stick, one end on Minor's shoulder, the other on mine, and we'd do the coolie trot, and giggle from success and elation. Once back in the shop we would hide in some dark storeroom and dine.

Cooking Food Will Smell

We had to be particularly careful of the kebihe snoopers if the food had to be cooked. Most of it was too dirty to use raw and take a chance on cholera. Most prisoners were allowed to have old cans or teapots for the boiling of water, as all drinking water had to be boiled to kill the germs. Minor and I had two healthy-size teapots, and when we set them on blacksmith forges to boil they were normally supposed to contain water and no suspicions would arise. However, let a spy catch a whiff of food from these pots, and the sky would fall. Usually we managed to find a Korean friend who would swear that the pot was his when a snooper raised the lid. Outside Koreans were allowed to prepare their own meals.

Sometimes the Nips became so interested in our teapot stews that they gave us curry, salt, or fish powder for seasoning, and always wanted a taste of the strange American concoctions. And our stews were good. Minor and I had many a laugh as our stomachs filled out while we hid in some dark corner licking up the hot meatless mulligans with chopsticks or a spoon made in the shop. "Our poor folks at home," we would say in allusion to Jap news stories about America not having any rice. "Yeah, we're lucky to be in Japan," we would giggle on a full stomach, "able to steal enough fish heads and cabbage to keep soul and body together." Perhaps my stomach would have shaken with more ironical laughter had I received news of just what was happening around my home community in America at the time. The war department had just informed my parents that the Japs had reported me as being alive. My pictures and name were seen in several newspapers, and many persons who had previously considered me as one of Mr. McBride's problem children were now praying for my safety and telling strangers what a wonderful boy I had been. I would have laughed especially had I known that an all-female cast was dedicating a Bataan three-act play to me back at Sul Ross College, where I had been a freshman in 1939.[4]

Pirates

When other prisoners got to stealing from the warehouse, it interfered with our racket. In the interest of safety we looked around for new sources.

The canal next to our shop was always half filled with houseboats and barges. The owners lived on board but were often away handling cargoes elsewhere. Having read pirate stories in our younger days, we got an itch to swarm over the sides and look for loot. One of us would stand ashore as a lookout while the other hand-walked a cable or poled out on a log to an anchored craft. Sometimes we would find a small bag of rice or a little sugar that the boatmen had snatched while unloading big ships from sugar islands — and now and then we would find oranges or other fruit.

In our second year at Yodogawa someone came to the shop for the platform scales. I think they were the only scales on the grounds. They were always out of order. Minor was the only man who could keep them in condition. We rolled the heavy things down to the canal, and there we beheld an open barge stacked high with golden oranges. Tons and tons of them. Minor whispered that we would get some or know the reason why. But people were around. Minor made an excuse that the scales had got out of order in our trundling them over the rough path. He returned for a wrench and a sack. We unscrewed nuts and tinkered for hours waiting for our chance. It was dark before we were alone temporarily. We scooped dozens of oranges into the burlap bag, and got away. There were too many to hide conveniently. We had to give away half of them to be safe — and we were scared for two or three days that someone would be careless with the peel and reveal our secret.

That Girl Bushy!

Near the rear of our shop was a gate opening on to a city street. It carried a steady stream of pedestrians and wheel traffic. When gasoline became scarce, trucks and cars were converted to charcoal burners for power. Charcoal had to be steamed to make gas. It has little force. Vehicles going up a sharp incline just outside the gate often had to stop while more gas was built up. Minor and I got to darting out and snatching daikons, radishes, squash and suchlike off the trucks. We could get only a handful because of our hurry.

One day Minor was hungrier than usual, so he ran out with a five-gallon can for a real supply. He began raking in small squash and cucumbers from the tail of a stalled truck. In the middle of the looting our little Japanese office girl, whom we called Bushy because of her fluffy hair, happened to step outside the gate. At sight of the frantically clawing Minor she let out a yip that could be heard all over Osaka.

"Quit that! Put it back!"

A well-dressed businessman heard and saw and shouted "*Koora*"* at Minor, but the sergeant was a determined character. He just wouldn't

*Hey, you!

quit. Bushy kept right on squalling. The businessman shook a fist. Other people stopped. I was waiting at the gate with a sack to take the loot. The truck started on. Minor came running back. He shoved the can into my hands. He put one hand against the back of Bushy's neck and the other over her mouth.

"You dry up, sister!" he ordered. "Don't give me away. You savvy?"

She nodded her clamped head. Her eyes twinkled. Minor let go. Bushy laughed hilariously, as if she liked being seized. I think Minor's action was one of the most foolhardy things I saw Americans commit in Japan. He could have been shot for touching the girl.

The Rice-Pipe Invention

Sometimes we prisoners were called on to unload plaited-fiber bags of rice from wagons. It was a ticklish process for us rice-eaters to cut a bag and steal handfuls; so someone invented the Yodogawa rice-pipe. The motions of putting handfuls of rice into a pocket is a peculiar gesture that can be recognized even at a distance. Besides, grains will spill and give one away. But with a slim metal pipe or hollow bamboo a foot or so long with one end sharpened — well, just jab the sharp end into the bag and let the pipe spill into your pants pocket. It's quick and not readily observed. One Yank invention always calls for another. It wasn't any time until a lot of us had sewed in pockets that went clean down to the knee. The fiber of the sack closes when the pipe is removed and nobody is the wiser. Try it sometime when you are starving.

There was a time in the second year when adventuresome prisoners dropped quietly out of the windows at night and wilted in the shadows. Some, growing bold, climbed the fence and roamed nearby streets, robbing stores. One night a venturesome sailor got caught in a store munching crackers and canned salmon that a thrifty Jap had hoarded. The story got around. A loud howl went up from some headquarters. Our local soldiers and kebihe were on the spot. After that the men on the shelves were counted every hour of the night. The sailor was given solitary confinement with two small rice-balls daily. In the daytime he was compelled to stand at attention for all the working hours just inside his barred door. After two months several prisoners signed a paper that they would watch him and not let him out again. With that promise he was permitted to leave confinement, on the ground that if he did do any more robbing the signers would be executed. He had contracted pneumonia during his confinement in the cold cell without blankets at night. He soon died.

West Point Bluffer

If a congressional committee could have visited us, heard our snarling, seen our every-man-for-number-one selfishness, they would have reported back home that we had degenerated into animals. There was plenty of evidence of it, but there was other evidence, too. Some men developed from irresponsibility and weaklings into staunchness.

Take some of the old professional soldiers who had drowned themselves in tropical rum for years; or old China hands, or Shanghai Marines, and sailors who had battled in every barroom from Vladivostok to Acapulco. Deprived of alcohol, many of them straightened up, saw themselves as others had seen them, and took to water only. I think forever.

Captain John Olson of Mississippi, our only West Point man, in spite of illness and a lack of cooperation from the prisoners, was a credit to America. Time after time he unselfishly saved enlisted men from beatings by climbing up to the Nips with his best bluff, brash as a recruit reporting to his officer. He would argue quietly, tell the Nips in their teeth that they were wrong even when they were shouting that the Imperial Japanese army was never wrong. The Nips hated to be found in poor judgment; they would see that here was a man who knew right, whose judgment was sound. By the very force of his character and decency Captain Olson would convince them. He always conducted himself as an officer and gentleman and by self-respect won our and the Japs' respect. It made us believe that West Point training had influence on mind and character.

I think it hurt Captain Olson more to see another American beaten than to be beaten himself, which he was. It was he and Major Reardon, our commander, and Captain Leslie Doane who initiated the practice of visiting the enlisted men daily at their work and passing out a few cheerful words, such as: "Morning, Mac. Morning Sergeant Minor. Don't do any more work than you have to keep from getting a beating. Keep yourselves fit. These slant-eyes are taking a beating in the Pacific now. We'll be getting out of here some of these times. Chins up!"

That Old Glory

A sailor named Spizzerio, from California, had hidden an American flag on his person when his ship went down in the Philippines. He kept it hidden. He hung on to it through thick and thin, discarding personal possessions to make room for it. Our gang of prisoners may never forget the Christmas Day that Captain Olson posted one of us on the barrack stairs to warn of a guard's approach, then took the flag and proudly displayed it for all to see. He said a few words to remind us that we were still Americans. Someone else recited the following lines from a bit of doggerel verse he had composed and I have never forgotten them:

> Dog eat dog and to hell with you,
> Do not, and never will rhyme,
> With Peace, Love and home,
> And cards at Christmas time.

You just didn't look to see if other men had tears in their eyes because you were blinded by your own. I think there was not a dry eye in the barrack. The view of that wonderfully colored Stars and Stripes was our Christmas treat. After V-J day and our liberation I saw Spizzerio on our homeward-bound ship still proudly displaying that flag.

It might be fitting to observe that men who did such things as Captain Olson and Spizzerio did — getting their minds off themselves by unselfishness for others — seemed to be the ones most certain to survive.

A Change of Sergeants

Our morale popped high when without warning our commander, Sergeant Hirose, was transferred. Men vowed that given half a chance he was one Jap they would kill. He was succeeded by Sergeant Tanaka. The new commander was different. He initiated two rest or *yasume* days a month in addition to the two days already allowed. He took all who were able to make the walk on a long hike into downtown Osaka, just for a change, and let us see the city. He repeated the gesture, and on the second hike he went so far that he became lost. To get back he loaded us on to a streetcar, paid our fares, and sent in a bill to the Yodogawa Works. Once he ordered us on a sit-down strike when factory officials refused his requisition for more food for us.

Sergeant Tanaka promised us that on our third trip downtown he would have the factory furnish a sightseeing bus; but he was just too good to last. He got the bounce. No doubt the factory owners put pressure on army headquarters.

Tanaka got more work out of us than the slave drivers did. He maintained discipline and insisted that all prisoners work hard. He kept an eye on us to see that we did. He was no fool. He would find Minor and me working industriously, as if it were our own war, but would look at our hands to see if it were bluff or if we had calluses. We did have calluses, even if it was from squeezing teapot handles. He presented me with a bottle of ketchup and a box of tea for being a good worker! And the next day he promoted me, who had been a buck private all through my army days, to be a private first class. He presented me with fancy red stripes and ordered that I wear them on my sleeves. A gesture, of course, to promote harder work. But even so he was human. Just too much of an idealist, in spite of efficiency, for hard-headed moneymakers.

Hashimoto Takes Over

In replacement of Tanaka, after his month with us, came Sergeant Hashimoto. He was a tough cavalryman. We didn't like his looks at first, but he proved to us that even a Jap can have a sense of humor. He knew the difference between the truth and a lie. He was just. He did not make idle promises, and the ones he did make he kept. He said from the first, and continually:

"If when you are guilty of stealing or any other misdemeanor, and I ask you for the truth and you lie, you will be punished severely. Remember never to lie to me. I will judge your case fairly. And I will punish never without reason."

A wonderful thing about Hashimoto was that he himself did all the punishing. He stopped indiscriminate knocking about. He would not permit the Beast to strike us. For months the Beast was docile to servility, trying to keep in the good graces of the much superior man, Sergeant Hashimoto. But when Hashimoto punished it was a real beating.

Because I could use the typewriter, I was called into Hasimoto's office to help our interpreter with lists of American names and to type letters which had been written in longhand by prisoners in hopes they would be mailed home. The interpreter wanted the letters typed so he could censor them more easily.

Since my return home I have been asked about the brief cards and letters received in America from prisoners of the Japanese. Particularly in New Mexico it seems that messages were received that sounded queer and beside the point, to such an extent that relatives doubted that they were written by their men, whose names were signed. We had to show our appreciation of the Japanese army in those communications. That may have been one angle of the oddness. Then no doubt the interpreter himself rewrote some of them, which would explain the queer Japanese phrasing.

While I was on the typing job Hashimoto learned that I could speak his language with some fluency. He asked me whether I would rather be in prison or out fighting. I answered, "Fighting." He told me about his fighting in China, saying that he lived under about the same conditions as we prisoners were enduring. It may have been his hardships in China that made him just and somewhat sympathetic with us — a rare trait, I think, to emerge from hardships. He asked me about the fighting on Bataan and when I told him of the harshness of the Death March he was disgusted with his countrymen. I remarked that he was the first Japanese to display such feeling. He smiled and wanted to know if I did not think him kinder than the Bataan Japanese. Truthfully I replied that he was.

Some of the letters I typed contained such phrases as, "We have a good commander now." The interpreter calling attention to this, Hashimoto beamed. He asked why the men wrote such things about the enemy. I told him that he was so much better than Hirose that the men could not help liking him. I believe this indirectly saved the lives of numerous Americans; for while Hashimoto did not strictly keep his stooges and the kebihe from stealing our supplies, he did make an effort to keep the camp clean and improve living conditions so that he could retain the American good opinion.

Jap Psychology

It is a loss of face for a Japanese officer to be talked about in public by his troops. Hashimoto and many others were so sensitive that they were afraid of being ridiculed behind their back by prisoners. This is supposedly bad for discipline, too. Major Noell, who spent many months in close contact with the Japs on Luzon, has explained this[5]: "All Nips who feel that their own face is in danger will torture their own men or prisoners. The Nips stand on their pride and it's slippery business at the best."

Hashimoto Learns Poker

Sergeant Hashimoto kept me off work several days to teach him and the interpreter American poker. Before the war the Japanese intellectuals had played poker in Tokyo — so Hashimoto informed me — and now the sergeant wanted to gain prestige by this means. I didn't tell him of the character status of the typical American who plays poker. I disliked the interpreter clear up into high G. He asked me to show him American card tricks. I told his fortune with cards; and turning up the ace of spades I told him it meant bad luck, the digging of a grave, and death. Two days before we had tried to poison this individual by putting what we thought was cyanide in his teapot. Sergeant Hashimoto did not like the fellow either and got a laugh out of the fortune telling. A year later the prisoners cursed happily when we heard this interpreter had died of tuberculosis. I thought of the Grumbler back at San Fernando, who hadn't any friends either.

Hashimoto decided that he wished to learn English as well as poker. With his flexible humor and being the practical joker that he was, he asked me to begin the lessons by first typing out all the American slang and cuss words I knew. Between us, the interpreter and I finally got it to Hashimoto what the words meant. He spent hours of smiling study. Soon he was roaring at the Beast and other stooges when they came into the office, "Get hell out, you sons-of-gun!" The interpreter would explain to the Beast, where-upon Hashimoto would double up with laughter at the man's confusion.

Having a good ear, Hashimoto learned words quickly. He got to con-cealing himself near working Americans and listening to their talk. Hear-ing a grumbling man use foul language, Hashimoto would spring out, grab the man by the arm, and demand, "Why you cuss me?" The astounded Yank would usually be quick enough to say that he meant it for a fellow worker, whereupon the sergeant would laugh and return to the office repeat-ing, "You damn jug-head so-and-so, you blasted rumdum." As likely as not he would bring the man to the office and have him swear some more. The man might get hours of rest — the reward for proficiency in profanity.

Japs Lax toward Emperor

Many months after working in Hashimoto's office I was reported to him as not working hard on my shop job. He asked if it were true. Aware of his passion for the truth, I explained that though I worked hard I was naturally slow, and also that I had never worked too hard even for the American army. I certainly did some rapid mental gymnastics. Hashimoto laughed and sent me back, telling me to work just as hard for the Emperor as I worked for Roosevelt.

The Japanese workmen asked a thousand and one questions about America. I told them that we did not have to salute or bow to our pres-ident, or anyone. They were amused and delighted. It made them skep-tical of the Japanese newspaper propaganda about Roosevelt being a cruel fiend and such like. To press the point I told them that our president was a kind, magnificent man who gave much time and money to sick children. I told them too that Roosevelt provided for his people better than their emperor provided for them. They nodded their heads believ-ingly. So the emperor suffered by comparison.

Helmets into Skillets

When inflation got its grip on Japan and it became more difficult to steal under the guards' noses, because they themselves were taking and selling all that they dared, I had to revert to the black market or starve. Minor and I had two Korean friends whom we called Pig and Dog on account of their animal faces. They were always sympathetic and would help us in any way they could.

Pig's wife had been exposed to Christianity in Korea, and out of the kindness of her heart she sent us almost daily a little jelly-cake made of sweet potato starch. They were tasteless and hard to swallow, but prisoners cannot be choosers and I manfully ate my share, for it was a gift from a kind heart. Pig, who had a large family, could not spare rice and hardly the cake.

Dog was an unusually illiterate fellow but clever. Almost daily he made something in our shop which he could smuggle out and sell. He knew that I could make things too. He brought in a cracked army helmet and told me he had picked it up in a nearby lot where defective helmets were temporarily discarded from a factory that made them. I looked it over and thoughtfully began to fashion it into something, which turned out to be a frying pan with a handle riveted on. Dog was delighted. He brought more helmets. I turned them into skillets and cooking pots. He peddled them on the black market and brought me rice. Some days Minor and I would eat more of this extra rice than other workers got on their allowed rations. Unfortunately I could no longer smuggle food into the barrack for the sick men.

War News Too Soon

When the Yanks started cleaning up on the Germans in Africa the Nips stopped newspapers from reaching us. From then on we were not supposed to know there was a war, but the Jap civilians had not been sufficiently indoctrinated. They kept telling us the news. When Italy surrendered Minor and I heard it ahead of the guards. We told our fellow Americans. The word got around swiftly over the factory compound. The guards traced it back to Minor. Hashimoto gave him a polishing off, trying to make him tell where he had heard it. Minor finally said he had overheard two unseen Japanese talking.

Lest it be assumed that I was the only American who knew Japanese, here is a good spot in which to remark that at least three others could speak it, one much better than I. He knew it before he ever reached Osaka as a prisoner.

As weeks made months and months made years of imprisonment, we grew more eager than ever to learn the news of the outside world, wondering if the Yanks were ever going to liberate us or if we were just going to stay there and grow old and rot. Men who were sent to the joke hospital across the Yodo River occasionally returned with tales and rumors which came from captives brought from Manila, Shanghai and Singapore, or from some flier who had been shot down, or a sailor rescued after a ship had been sunk. But we were hungry for more authentic news. It became an obsession with some of us. Officers and others waited anxiously each evening for the three or four of us who spoke Japanese to make our reports.

Through bribery several men working together were able to get the *Osaka Mainichi,** printed in English, smuggled to them. Private Mike Campbell of Detroit, Michigan, and others finally got a system working so smoothly that a well-paid Nip would quit work, jump on his bicycle, and pedal to town for the *Mainichi* just as it came off the morning press. By noon the paper would be in our barrack. My learning of Japanese included the sound language alphabets, Katakana and Hirokana, and also a few of the ideographic military terms, so that I could fairly well decipher the mystery of Japanese-language papers picked up from trash piles. A wet and wind-blown sheet became a real find.

"All Cowards' Day"

In all factories and such places in Japan, the working people were always called together on the eighth day of each month to hear a pep talk and praise of the emperor in order to speed up war production. We prisoners dubbed it "All Cowards' Day" because it was also in celebration of the opening of the war and their Pearl Harbor "victory." Minor and I appreciated these *Banzai*† meetings because most of the Japanese left the shop and gave us two hours or so to ourselves. The majority of

*Osaka Daily, a newspaper.
†"Long Live the Emperor."

workers dodged the meetings and went off for tea-sipping or shopping. But Minor and I were free to catch up on some of our sabotaging and other secret activities.

On the eighth of a springtime month we were sitting at the street gate — it was no longer guarded — hoping that a vegetable truck would pass so we could snatch something to eat. The Missourian, who was a good-looking chap even garbed as a prisoner, had a way with women. We had a couple of Korean slave girl acquaintances — they worked in the main factory office — who occasionally brought us beans from the black market or gave us a wink or a smile. This day Cho Cho and Pata came along the street hand in hand and started smiling and giggling when they saw us. I suppose they were lonesome, or were like many a girl in any land where all the healthy men except draft dodgers have gone off to war. They stopped in front of us, gouged their toes in the dust, and said hello in their language. They asked us if we were married or had American "*koybitas*"* waiting for us back home. We said no and they informed us that they liked us. Then came questions about dancing and school life and kissing. We offered to teach them about school life but they put a finger on lips and repeated the Jap word for "keep this a secret," walked away from us, looking back to smile and see if we were watching. We did not come across Pata and Cho Cho for months but saw them daily, without speaking, as we carried water from a hydrant beneath their office window. Occasionally they left a bowl of rice and motioned for us to take it.

Tidal Wave Hits Prison

In September 1944, a tidal wave came in suddenly from the sea, smashed the seawall close to the factory, and flooded our whole industrial section of Osaka north of the Yodo River.

As the waters came roaring we prisoners were rushed into our two-story barrack. From the windows we watched the inundation of the Nip civilian homes and factories. As darkness fell the waters rose higher. It got to the electric power plant in the Yodogawa works. We saw light-

*Sweethearts.

ning flashes as transformers sizzled and burned. We knew the saltwater would ruin every one of our poorly insulated motors. It was a big show for us, super-sabotage by Nature, that would slow down the Nip war production all over the district far more than we could ever hope to do.

When the water rose higher it got into a warehouse where the factory supply of carbide was stored. The water seeped into the loosely sealed cans and formed a gas, so that there was explosion after explosion and the buildings began to burn.

Several of our guards were trapped in the city and could not reach our barrack. The Beast was among them. The handful of kabihe who remained were forced to join us in our crowded room. The water soaked the rice stores in the kitchen. Sergeant Hashimoto used his head. He ordered the great pots of rice be cooked to keep it from spoiling. We weren't hungry during the flood. The Nips were so scared and we were so delighted with all the destruction that they turned to us to solve their problems.

They sent us out next morning to locate boats and rafts and help with rescue and salvage. The sea was still too high to repair the breached wall, and as the regular tides came in more water poured through. We prisoners were largely unguarded and had plenty of freedom. Why didn't we escape? Where would we have gone?

A lot of the boys rowed around looking for warehouses and storage dumps. Minor and I picked up a lot of soap which was by then a scarce article in Japan. We also rescued from a watery grave a bag of beans and some vegetables, thus preventing their falling into the hands of snatchers. We poled into our deserted shop and docked at some high shelves and hid the stuff.

Bands of coolies were running around stealing. They hadn't any patriotism. It should be a lesson to rich overlords in any land to see that the coolie class is elevated to literacy and treated with economic justice so that they will be more likely to remain loyal in emergencies. Coolies were not only stealing, but were fighting and knifing. It was a nice slice of anarchy.

Pata and Cho Cho Again

When the waters subsided somewhat a few factory workers were on hand to help with cleaning up mess. Minor and I were sent to the shop to run an electric pump in an attempt to remove some of the water around the valuable machinery. We were left for days by ourselves. Most of the time we did not run the pump, readying as an excuse if we were caught that the motor had become hot and because of the oil shortage we just had to let it cool or it would be ruined.

We were safely hiding in the rear of the shop, boiling some of our beans over a rigged-up charcoal fire, when we heard a rapping at a door. Startled, thinking it might be a guard, we hastily hid our beans and got ready to lie, run or commit murder if we had to.

We opened the door. There stood our girl friends, Cho Cho and Pata. They had seen us enter the shop from the front and had waded water waist deep to come to the rear door in hopes of not being seen fraternizing with us. They had been wet and cold in their office and hoped that we had a fire so they could dry out. These two particular Korean girls were Jap citizens and we mere prisoners did not dare refuse them. We did not like the idea, though, because our minds were on beans and not girls.

After a two-man conference, the man from the Show-me State and I decided that if we locked the doors the girls would not be caught fraternizing with us. It was impossible for anyone to come upon us without wading and stumbling over machinery in the big front shop and being heard. So we moved our stove to a secure corner and just kept on boiling our beans while the girls dried out. Minor and I had used some of our new-stolen soap to clean up. Perhaps the girls found us presentable, for they began to talk pleasantly.

They sang Santa Lucia with Japanese words and we hummed tunes we knew to see if they were familiar to our guests. Before they left they told us we must meet them the next day as they had something from America to show us. Minor and I joked about which girl was whose, and remarked that if the Beast caught us, wouldn't he have a hemorrhage! Also we wondered what they might have from America and guessed everything from a bobby pin to checkers.

The girls returned early the next morning with a guitar, a package that proved to be their lunch, and a 1939 issue of a movie magazine called *Film Fun*. They had been using it for their fashion plate. They showed us pictures of actresses and asked if they had succeeded in fixing their hairdos about the same way. Minor and I were so embarrassed that our faces were red. They remained most of the day with us. They informed us they were not bad girls, that they did not like the war either, and that they were going to help us because they liked America and felt so sorry for us because we were not receiving letters from our sisters, mothers and fathers. We told them that if they would not endanger our necks by coming back, we would take them some later magazines after the war and teach them how to dance. They smiled.

Japs Lose Morale

With the work of reconstruction in the factory area, prison life turned to monotonous, hungry, blank and lonesome days. The Nips were morose and gloomy, their morals on the toboggan. What laughter and smiles there had been were dried up. They began to admit grudgingly that the war was hopeless. Many students of the Orient had asserted that the Japanese would never lose their spirit and determination to fight to the last grain of rice. I do not think this is true of the Japanese industrial workers. When the war ended, Lieutenant General Kanji Ishihara wrote for the Tokyo daily newspapers[6]: "The greatest reason for the Japanese defeat was the deterioration of the nation's morality."

The Japs' mood had an effect on us. Of the 137 remaining Americans half were tough customers, physically or mentally or both, fighting it out on their own legs for survival, but even they were depressed. And the sick were worse. They needed more waiting on. I think the men missed tobacco more than ever though the meager issue of cigarettes had been stopped long before this. Now, even the Japanese were getting only three a day. But we continued to keep clean, and yasume days were still observed, with the guards passing out shears for us to clip one another's hair. Clipped craniums aren't pretty sights.

Among the many Nips frequently entering the factory on business was a Jap who said he had formerly lived at San Antonio, Texas, and had been a bootlegger for the soldier boys. He could sling all the American slang in the book and then some. He talked freely of the war, expressing the opinion that the "damned heathen Japs were getting licked on all sides."

"I hope it's all over right pronto," he said, "so I can get back to San Anton' and business." One morning he came to me jabbering excitedly.

"Tojo has surrendered Saipan! They've booted him out of the premier-ship. They've put in Koiso. He'll run the whole show, believe me. He'll give the skids to the generals and put in new ones. I bet the blasted Nips win the war yet," he added disgustedly.

When I asked about the war in Europe he said the Japs weren't printing much. We weren't getting the copy of the *Mainichi* anymore. Through my grapevine connections with American prisoners in other sec-tions of Osaka we sometimes got a few words of news. Now and then one driving a truck past the gate would yell something, such as, "The Allies have about got the Germans licked." The truck guard would shut him off instantly.

Higher-Ups Are Doubtful

By the winter of 1944–45 the Japanese higher-ups did not think too glamorously of their chances, it appeared to us. They let a cat out of the bag by feeble attempts to improve prison conditions. Comman-der-Sergeant Hashimoto was removed and we received a nasty half-pint, effeminate sergeant named Yamamoto. The Japanese propaganda radio in a program sent to America during this time reported[7]:

> Japan is ready to do anything she can to improve the lot of Allied prison-ers. We hope the enemy will in turn recognize the Japanese generosity for making such a noble decision.

All prisoners were stripped to the bones one day while Colonel Morada, in charge of all Osaka prison camps, inspected our emaciated frames and made us a speech.

"You complain of not receiving proper treatment. We feed you as much rice as we give our little schoolchildren. You are ungrateful. We let you take a bath almost every day, while my own daughter can bathe in warm water but once in ten days."

We wanted to yell that speech back down his throat. About a week later our rations were increased somewhat but not enough to keep hunger away and cure our ills. By this time, all our men who had had malaria and dysentery had died. Several had died of tuberculosis. Eight men were lying on the shelves dying of this disease, though sometimes they were forced to go out for light work. We all lived in the barrack with these men.

In this last winter we had been given more stoves but the factory owners refused to supply fuel. Sometimes our fires would all be out. If we could get a little kindling we had no matches. Prisoners never were permitted to possess them. There were coke and coal piles near the blast furnaces, and passing prisoners would snatch up a pocketful. The kebihe had learned by now that we were such thieves it was more profitable to let us take in stuff and make us hand over money for not reporting us. Yes, Japan seemed to be letting down, disintegrating.

Minor and I and several others got on to an idea for a bit of private heat. From electric elements out of parts stolen in the electric shop we made gadgets and put them between the outer and inner walls of the barrack and connected them, after lights out, with the lamp cords. We could keep our feet warm by sleeping with them against the wall spots. The Nips never did get on to it. Sometimes half-freezing men would take turns through the nights lying for a while with their soles on the warm dot.

Methodist Preaching

Along with their many gestures to gain our regard — in hopes we would write letters home to influential men asking their influence with Roosevelt in calling off the war, actually! — the Japs now permitted us to have one Christian ceremony. Two Japanese Methodist ministers were admitted to the barrack. As they were subjects of the emperor we all had to rise and bow and salute.

To our surprise, one of the ministers spoke out in perfect English, telling us that he was a graduate of Southern Methodist University at Dallas, Texas. He led us in hymn singing, then preached a sermon with the proper modulation of voice. It was a taste of home for many. The service ended without any person going forward at the call, and we stood again and bowed and saluted as the ministers left.

Free Americans Up There!

American bombers started work over Japan in the autumn of 1944 and the people were getting nervous. There had been several practice alarms in Osaka. When the sirens turned loose, we prisoners were instructed to report to our work leaders, then assemble in the yard by the barrack and go into the open splinter-shelter.

One morning a B-29 slipped in over Osaka before the alarm could be given. At first it was so high we could not see it, yet the hum of the motors and the air vibrations were so clear that it seemed to be a ghost. Then it came into sight and I got my first glimpse of that wonderful machine. It sailed along in a straight course while little black puffs of Jap flak hunted for it. But the shots were always below and behind. This was a happy moment for us all, a significant moment. We were the nearest to free Americans that we had been since the surrender of Bataan. Some of the men murmured, "Free Americans up there!"

Osaka was not bombed when planes first started hitting Japan. It was other cities that caught it, one after another. When the Yank planes were anywhere over the home islands the alarm was spread to Osaka by telephone. Cho Cho and Pata were the telephone girls in the main office. They always received the messages. I carried more water than we needed, from the spigot under their window, just to hear them rattling off the news that was so good to us. Once they said to me, "Fifty of your friends over Nagoya — don't you wish you could see them."

A few days after that lone B-29 I saw ten more flying in formation. The Nips scattered like hens from a hawk. We prisoners howled with welcome. There was no bombing. Soon afterward single B-29's started flying over Osaka. They would circle an hour or more. War of nerves. They would get the Nips out of bed and send them scurrying to the cold bomb shelters with armloads of possessions. The people would try to sleep in the crowded places, or on the streets. Then when hopes had risen that there would be no bombs the high explosive would begin to fall.

The detonations might be five or six miles from Yodogawa but we could hear the blasts and rumbles and feel the earth tremble. We could go cheerfully to sleep then. But the succeeding day it would not be pleasant to work with the sleepy and disgruntled Japs who gave us the mean eye and cursed Roosevelt, America and the *B ni ju ku*.* They spoke with respect of the big planes, though. It was plain to all what a superior craft

*B-29 bombers.

they were, for in the occasional attacks on the B-29's the Japs saw their own planes shot down, unable to reach the big high-flying American birds.

The Humorous Earthquake

One afternoon around the time Tokyo was first being heavily bombed, Minor and I were shifting pipe outside the shop when one of the frequent earthquakes began pitching the earth around with the hoopla of a bucking bronc. A Jap mechanic, whom we called the Kibitzer because he was always peering and meddling in other people's affairs, came running out of the shop. Just for the hell of it the Missourian and I yelled "B-29, *B ni ju ku!*" The Kibitzer relayed the yell to the shop crowd and Nips came boiling out. The Kibitzer, like a worried lieutenant, began sighting into the sky with his slide rule to estimate the height of the supposed planes. The quake became more industrious, throwing people down. It was the most violent that I went through in Japan. People were crawling and scurrying on hands and knees like ants, thinking that it was bombs doing the mischief.

Minor and I guffawed and rocked. Smokestacks began to tumble and buildings shivered and groaned. We caught hold of metal posts set in concrete to keep upright. Electric wires broke and sputtered. Loading cranes waved and bowed. Building began to split. The Nips wormed behind anything that would protect them. We saw them hand-shading their eyes in the best Lone Indian tradition, searching the sky for the dreaded bombers, but Minor and I were all at once fresh out of laughter, for we let go the iron posts and the violent motions threw us rolling.

City Afraid of Fire

Pasted all over Osaka were large posters depicting balls of fire and leaping flames drawn to look like President Roosevelt's head. There was some subtle hint of humor about them. The Nips would bring them in to show us, and we would grin. There were warning sentences that the cruel American president intended to burn the city and the people's homes and that they must be instantly ready to fight fires.

On March 12, 1945, we Yodogawa prisoners managed to get several newspapers and other up-to-the-minute information as to how, when, and where our bombers were hitting. We could see that our fliers were working right down the Pacific side of Japan as they progressed from Tokyo. We made a guess that it would be Osaka's turn in two or three days. When we went to the shop Minor and I proudly pointed to Mr. Roosevelt's flaming pictures and told the Nips that in two days — we held up two fingers for emphasis — Osaka would catch it. "They'll burn your town to ashes," we boasted.

What a break we got on that! At about 11:30 on the night of March 14, after we prisoners had got to sleep, a bedlam of sounds awoke us. Sirens — big, little, shrill, bellowing, moaning, even weeping it seemed — broke across the bay in the city of Kobe. Osaka joined in the tumult. Before all of us prisoners could be herded down to the splinter-shelter, known as the air-raid pen, planes were overhead.

How Did the Fliers Know?

Clouds were low over Osaka. We could not see the planes at first. Suddenly great flares were dropped. Our barrack, the shops and foundries, were lighted up. It appeared as if the planes were using our barrack as a hub. As if they knew where to bomb away from it!

Just west of us a mass of planes became visible. They came right over our prison, as if saying "Howdy, guys." The terrific hum and roar shook our insides. I was to hear one of the fliers later say that the planes came down under the clouds by the use of radar.

Just beyond us the planes raised slightly over Osaka and we saw fire bombs hit factory roofs, saw little sprays of fire bounce like rubber balls and spread in gorgeous blossoms, saw flames start up in ever-spreading circles.

Some of the bouncing fire fell into the Yodo river and went floating down to the sea. Jap anti-aircraft guns split the night and their falling flak peppered the roofs around us.

With all the other confusion we prisoners were yelling like madmen. Hooray for Uncle Sam! We had not until then seen American planes in action since Bataan and Corregidor, now so very long behind us. We hoped the incendiaries would burn Yodogawa out of existence, and we didn't care much who got killed.

The three-hour raid ended and our guards came to see how we had fared. We expected them to be murderous and beat us, but they were grinning sheepishly and were still frightened.

Back in the barrack, some of us stood at the windows far into the night. A burning city is a magnificent sight.

They Taste the American Pill

There was no work the following day. Many of the factory laborers were sifting the ashes of their homes to salvage what they could. Streetcar lines were choked with debris and could not carry the workers. For a while there was no current, until lines could be tied in with the Kobe power plants. Osaka was in dreadful confusion. The raid had destroyed the best of what the Japanese had built in the years since the great destructive earthquake of 1923. Most of the estimated 4,600 factories were burned, blown up or damaged, along with the arsenal and gas works. Japan's No. 1 manufacturing city was largely in ruins.

For three days the city was under martial law. We prisoners were kept in the barrack-room under heavy guard. Perhaps the Nips were fearful that we might break out and join their roving bands of coolies, who combed the wreckage, looting, murdering, fighting over spoils as they had after the flood, only much worse. From our window we could see groups of people in the street below weeping together as at a funeral.

Some opportunist slipped what was reported to be a ton of counterfeit ten-yen notes on the black market. They flooded the city. I got several of them later; they all bore the same serial number.

With the market destroyed, our supply of vegetables was cut off. Shut up in our room we suffered from hunger, but there was one consolation: One of our nastier guards, named Adachi, a pal of the Beast, came walking into the compound wheeling the remains of his burned, tireless bicycle, his wife and children pitifully trailing with a few handfuls of scorched possessions they had retrieved from their home. Adachai's hair was crisped, his face burned, his clothes dirty and torn. He asked our American prison medical men for aid. He was the Nip who, a month before, had been responsible for making all prisoners go without two meals. He was the man who had subjected us to long periods of standing at attention while he beat various ones. He had cut off our meager supply of salt and had caused the stoves to be removed from the barrack. Now he came crawling, asking for salve and for permission for him and his family to live with us for a while.

A popular American magazine reported later that twenty percent of Osaka had been destroyed in this raid. Three hundred planes carried over four million pounds of explosives and incendiaries over the city, blowing up the arsenal and most of the factories.[8]

Kobe Has a Show

As the remains of Osaka were being cleaned up our neighboring Kobe, one of the great shipbuilding centers of the empire, caught it from our bombers. On the night of March 17, the planes were attacking about ten minutes after the first screams of the sirens.[9] Most of us prisoners were rushed to the "death pen." I was left inside the barrack to carry out blankets in case the planes took another rap at Osaka and we were hit. From a window I watched the edge of the bay as countless tons of high explosives and incendiaries fell along the Kobe harborfront. I saw explosions and big fires break out. The fires would die down, the spots apparently would be rebombed, and the flames would break out anew. It was a great show, the culmination of three years for Americans, the emperor's nation being blasted. It was almost worth the price of admission.

For the next two days thousands of homeless people carrying their pitiful bundles and babies straggled past our barrack.

Yodogawa factory soon resumed work, on a limited scale. It lacked coal and other fuels. Thousand of houseboats and barges in the river and canals had been burned in the raid. Without such transportation the few industrial places that remained could get materials, and were crippled beyond immediate recovery.

If our fellow working Japs were an indication, the nation was in black discouragement. Hundreds left the area to move their families into the country and mountainous places for safety. They looked beaten. And our punches were continued. Three days after the first raid a few flights of Grumman fighters from naval aircraft carriers pasted Kobe again. Six or so big anchored balloons floated over Osaka as a trap for low-flying planes, but eight of the Grummans peeled off from the flight, sailed over the city regardless of balloons, and set many millions of legs to scissoring through the streets.

We Make Another Prophecy

In these bad days for the Nips we had to keep our eyes open, for the Japs were sore and touchy and we half expected them to snatch up poles or irons and attack us. The Koreans were quietly happy.

Some of the foremen tried to pile work on Minor and me. We balked and sat down in a corner and sulked along with the native and Korean workers, and Suzuki was away. The office engineer got a whiff of what we were doing. He came in and pleaded with us to help center some holes in expensive rollers which unskilled workmen had all but ruined beyond our correction. We said:

"What's the use? This whole shop and everything in it is going to be blown to hell in one month. Why work? We'll all be killed in the raid."

The engineer must have remembered our prediction on March 12 that Osaka would be bombed in two days, for he looked worried, scratched his head, and said, "Work at your own convenience, honorable prisoners."

This time our prediction fell short. It was two months before Yodogawa was bombed to destruction. By then all the American prisoners were gone, including Minor and myself.

I wonder how the Yanks knew that?

Roosevelt's Passing

In the succeeding days word came that President Roosevelt had died. I think the news reached us within hours. A coolie told me. He said a man named "Toe-Rue-Mahn" was the new Number One man in

America. I did not recall having ever even heard the name. I hurried with the news to the other Americans. It spread swiftly. There was no excitement. Each man as he heard took on an expression of blank surprise and shock. In time we learned the hour of the funeral. That night in the barrack we all stood for a moment and someone said a few words. We regretted his loss but we felt that the war would go on.

We Eat Horse Corn

With the cities torn and bleeding, food was scarce again. Even the black market was letting us down. Minor and I knew the war could not last much longer. We weren't going to starve to death now. We watched the kitchen warehouse without seeing any rice coming in. The Yodogawa pipeline wasn't working anymore. I got so hungry I couldn't sleep. Hungry prisoners prowled and grumbled all night.

There was one source Minor and I had neglected: the grain boxes where carthorses were fed in the compound. We began to snitch corn from the animals. Sometimes it had been slobbered on, but what the hell? It tasted all right when it had been boiled soft and fat, and crunched okay when it was toasted. I got so I was ashamed to look an honorable horse in the face.

Other prisoners thought of the horse feed and stole so much that the horses weren't able to do their pulling. Guards caught several prisoners with the grain and the cart men were warned to watch their animal feed.

Minor and I discovered another wareroom. With the help of Chief Ben Dow, a sailor, and Corporal Morfvedt of the Marines, we issued ourselves two bags of something that proved to be wheat. It had got singed when Osaka burned but had been resacked, and though it was damp it turned out to be number-one chow after it was washed a few times.

Other prowling prisoners found our hole in the wall and likewise issued themselves wheat by the bags. By the spring of 1945 we guests of the emperor had learned the little knack of hiding anything from our hosts, from a sen to a sack of grain. In our spare moments Minor and I had built a false wall in the rear of an air-raid hole. Here we set up our smokeless charcoal stove and secretly cooked our wheat. Boiled á la teapot it was quite agreeable to the stomach and stopped our losing more weight. Perhaps I have overlooked mentioning that by now the beri-beri cases were improved, including my own. We slept better. There was laughter at times. During the wheat harvest you could hear men with satisfied bellies ask and giggle, "Have you tried Wheaties?"

The Nips eventually discovered the hole in the wall and soberly deduced that somebody was short on wheat. After some clever sleuthing they decided that the Americans were the guilties. Some of us eventually got beatings, but they were to the inward amused tune of, "O, have you seen the hole in the warehouse wall?"

Our chins were distinctly up. We surmised that we would not be here much longer. The breakup, for our bunch, came sooner than anticipated.

Disloyal to the Emperor

On an early day in May, right out of the blue all prisoners were lined up on the cinders by the camp commander and the Beast. All of us whose names had never been jotted down on the Beast's list as being willing workers were handpicked from the approximately 265 who remained, and were stood to one side.

Various lists were checked and men shifted. I was placed next in a group of individuals who had never perspired much working for the captors. Charges were read out against us — quarrelsomeness with other Americans, suspicion of sabotage, disloyalty to the emperor (really) — and about everything else Nips could think of, without there being openly expressed evidence against us.

There were secret lists, too, and it burned up some of the men because they couldn't find out what was written against them. But the office had kept blacklists, and there were men on them who weren't much in favor around Yodogawa. Definitely I wasn't on any list of men who had tried to honey the guards for personal benefit. Nor was Minor.

On the sixth of May we managed to obtain a copy of the *Mainichi* with the news of Germany's surrender. That evening at roll call we were about to burst with happiness when our camp commander faced us and made a speech. It was simple. He just read off eighty names, including mine, and informed us that we were being sent away from Yodogawa to a place he was forbidden to tell us. That was all the information. There wasn't any more.

Last Day at Yodogawa

Early in the morning of May 8, 1945, we eighty men were marched out of Yodogawa, without tears. Come what would, we were glad to leave this damned spot of two and a half years imprisonment.

I didn't know it but I had been sentenced to coal mines on Kyushu* Island to the south.

I am not at liberty at the time to tell why I was sentenced. But one thing I can say: A part of the reason was to separate Sergeant Willis B. Minor of Missouri, U.S.A., and me — so far apart that we could not communicate. He was sent to the extreme northern islands.

As we eighty marched out of the compound, Minor and a few others slipped near to wave and grin a last goodbye. But Minor got home. I have received letters from him at his Missouri home since we landed on U.S. soil.

*The southern and third largest island of the Japanese Empire, about 300 air miles from Okinowa.

Chapter VII

Slavery in Coal Mines

The March of the Eighty from the Yodogawa works was straight into the center of Osaka. As we tramped along, in step again like soldiers, I saw miles of the city which were nothing but bricks and ashes. The sight was satisfying, though I realized the horrible waste of lives and property.

At the city's subway station we had to wait two hours for a special car to transport us. We stood in line and watched the people. I saw no smiles. A crowd swarmed around us with harsh, jerky talk. They weren't trying to give us cigarettes or food. The guards with bayonets pushed them back.

I kept looking for a European face. Occasionally I saw among the slant-eyes what appeared to be white or European countenances, but on inspection they turned out to be half-breed Japanese or the light-skinned aborigines, the Ainu, from northern Hokkaido Island.

The subway carried us to Kobe. From there by surface car we went into the mountains behind the city. Leaving the car we straggled along in an irregular line to a charming little terraced village. The surrounding country looked like a well-cared-for park in America. It was a pleasant sight to our slum-factory-weary eyes. We learned that it had been the estate of a British business tycoon before the war. We arrived at a high board wall with barbed wire on top. We were at another prison camp. The guards crowded us through a gate, passing out a few farewell slaps and thuds with rifle butts.

White Men Face to Face

Within the new compound we were counted and assigned to barracks, with rooms larger and cleaner than those we had left. After a few minutes we were given the liberty of the camp. Other prisoners were waiting for us, and for the first time in two and a half years we were face to face with strangers, white men. It was sort of unbelievable and we stared curiously.

As we soon learned, there were about seventy Americans, 200 Australians, 400 British and 200 Dutch. They were bonier and more starved than us. They told a story of imprisonment since the fall of Singapore which was similar to ours. Only, these men had been unable to work much because they were where they could not steal food and keep up their strength. Even to our sickly crowd they were pitiful. They had heard no news of the war. How their eyes opened when we told them that Germany was being occupied by the Allies! They simply absorbed us eighty Americans. "This is our happiest day since Singapore," they told me time and again, with helpless tears flowing down their cheeks, as I spilled news to them for two hours.

This was Kawasaki prison. After two days all of us, foreigners and Americans, were lined up on the parade ground with our rags and scraps of junk packed for traveling. The eighty of us were herded strictly apart from the other Americans. The thousand prisoners were jubilant. We gabbled that the war was about over and we would be given medical attention and better food.

White Woman

Twenty Australians were attached to our eighty to make an even hundred. Taken into Kobe on interurban cars to what appeared to be the center of the city, we were unloaded for transfer to a train. While we waited at the station, close beside the track, a car going in the opposite direction to our route pulled in. I saw a white woman inside, the first in years. Before my staring could become rude she rose and came quickly to the window right before me. She was blond, dainty and nice. She leaned with her hands on the window bars and smiled and spoke:

"Haloo!" she said with an odd accent. "Keep your cheen up!"

One of the white Russians who had been living in Japan, I supposed, but a real honest-to-goodness white woman. It must have been sheer pride in kinship of race that caused her to speak.

We Travel to Kyushu

We boarded the train, and as we traveled southwest along the Pacific coast of Honshu Island, we saw many spots where our bombers had hit. The Japanese countryside of rice paddies and green hills was beautiful. Finally the shades were pulled down to shut off our scenic viewing. The car was packed. Not all had seats. We traveled until late into the night. I peeked out under the shades for a long time and saw huge fires burning in the darkness where the shapes of houseboats and barges could be seen on water.

Sometime in the night we transferred to a side-tracked car, and there we sat for two whole days. The railroad had been bombed and we had to wait for repairs. We were given rice and vegetables three times a day. Jammed in the crowded space, men because restless and quarrelsome. We saw other prisoners, of different nationalities, marched past and loaded into other coaches. There were frequent air raids in these two days, within hearing but not in sight.

When we moved southward we passed through Hiroshima, which was to gain fame within a few weeks as the first atomic-bombed city on earth. Perhaps the world has wondered why it was chosen for the doubtful honor from all the cities of Japan. My only answer — and it may be wrong — is that it had the reputation of being the most physically and morally dirty and evil city in the empire; and that, I understand, it had no prisoners of war. A Yankee-picked Sodom and Gomorrah perhaps. When I saw it after the A-bombing, the contents of a glass factory on a mountainside had melted and flowed down like a vast icicle.

We crossed by tunnel under the narrow strait from Honshu Island to Kyushu Island and the train kept on to our destination, a town called Oita, which we realized with consternation was right in the heart of the coal-mining district.

We Enter the Mines

Our new prison, called Fukuoka 27, was a slave camp, nothing less. The daily fare was meager rice and a bitter soup made from green weeds and vegetable tops. There were numerous mines and prison groups in

the area. The mine we Americans were assigned to had not been operated for a long time. I was told that the last people to work in it had
been German prisoners during World War I.

This was our daily schedule: out of bed before daylight, a handful
of boiled rice and the bitter soup, then a march of three miles to the
shaft. Work shifts were alternated, ten days in daytime, ten at night. In
those first days we seemed always to hike those three miles in mud and
rain. In the mine we carried electric headlamps on our foreheads and the
battery on our backs. The shoes of most of us were worn out and we
bound scraps of canvas around our feet. We would enter the black hole
by the uncertain light of the headlamps and go slipping and half falling
down the narrow, twisting path for four hundred meters — more than
thirteen hundred feet — to the numerous chambers where we moiled and
labored.

At first only Americans went underground for the hard mining. The
starved Australians and English just couldn't take what we stronger Yanks
could. Besides, the Americans were putting on air raids over Kyushu at
the time, almost daily and hourly; and working us below was one way
the Japs got even. To the Japanese, Americans were the most unpopular
people on earth just then.

In the mine we were associated with about the lowest form of
humanity that can be imagined — a type of mixed-race Japanese citizens
of Chinese, Korean, Malayan, Javanese, and Indonesian blood. The Japs
do not particularly care for mixed breeds. They were ignorant and brutal. I toiled with a crew of four other Americans. We five had to mine
thirty tons of coal a day before we were allowed to walk out, drag the
three miles to camp, grab our slop, sleep a few hours, then repeat.

I knew nothing whatever of mining. I have learned since then that
we were using a method which is common. We bored holes into the face
of the coal with air drills. The mixed-breed workers put in dynamite or
blasting powder, I do not know which. We Americans were not supposed to handle the stuff lest we commit sabotage. Detonation caps were
set with wires off some distance around a corner to comparative safety.
We touched the wires to our batteries, and blasted the coal down. Then
we set to work, into smoke and powder gases, and broke up the big
chunks with our picks and pulled down loose stuff and rocks from the
roof.

The coal was a soft, steam-producing variety of fuel. We loaded it into wooden boxes. Two men breasting against a box pushed it over an uneven track of old and rotting logs for about a hundred yards to steel cars. The boxes had no wheels. The log-skid way was downslope, otherwise we could never have slid the loaded boxes. The coal was transferred by hand into the steel cars, which were hauled up a long ramp to the surface by a grunting, hissing steam locomotive.

When we got a steel car full we were supposed to have thirty tons. The estimate was by bulk and not by weight — an important factor when we had learned the tricks of the trade. With the car loaded we were at liberty to leave — climbing, half-crawling at times, up that thirteen hundred feet of slippery path. The terrific labor of the long shifts pulled me down rapidly.

Coal Falls on Americans

Accidents happened every day in the mine, to the Japanese as well as to us prisoners. The coal vein was of uneven thickness. Here it would be no more than four feet high, a few yards farther along it would be higher than our heads. Often we had to quit mining and carry poles or small logs to prop up the roof. We had to carry these at a run. Once our group had to bore a hole for blasting in a patch of roof over our heads. The ceiling was not completely propped. We five held the heavy power drill to the hole, all of us bunched together. A great chunk of coal turned loose. It knocked us to the floor. My four companions were injured. I was able to walk unaided, so I went for help. The guard would not give permission for the four to be carried out. He ordered me to continue with my work. I told him the men must be given assistance, that more coal might fall and kill them. The old Japanese dread of being wrong before an American worked again. He made no objection, beyond some howling, when I proceeded to help my buddies out.

The accident taught me caution. I hated the underground job. I felt that if we had to work here through the winter none of us would be alive by spring. I shuddered to look at my frame, all joint-knobs now under the skin. My old resolution to survive came back and prodded me on. I refused to run anymore at the prop carrying. When the group failed at the end of twelve hours to have thirty tons, I signed the release book myself, showing the required amount of work accomplished. It was taking a ticklish chance of being found out by the soldier guards at the mine mouth. The armed men never ventured into the dangers of the mine, but were always at the top to catch work-beaters. Somehow I was never caught at the faking — "protective influence" again?

At the end of ten days I went to the night shift, along with the other four of the group. The others were Private First Class George Bestic of Los Angeles; Private Victor Dengelegi of Pennsylvania; Chief Rebufatti, a sailor from Illinois; and a fifth man, usually some Englishman or Australian dragged from a sickbed who was so weak he was only underfoot. Each group had a honcho, or leader. Because I was the strongest and spoke the language, I had been chosen for the job by the four, and I continued. The honcho's job, aside from the regular duties, was to receive instructions about the work from the Nip bosses and to make the proper bows and salutes when mine or army officials came around. Fortunately the inspectors did not often show up at night. They were afraid of the old mine with its dangerous ceilings, rotting props, and gas-laden air — and also afraid of a pick in the hands of a prisoner. The night shifts had a little more freedom, though they still had to get out the thirty tons for each group.

More Sabotage

In the darting lights and shadows of the mine, my tough group whispered together of ways for sabotage. Whether we did this with motives as pure as the driven snow — for our country — or selfishly, for our own benefit, it might be difficult for a psychologist to say. You can take your choice. There wasn't much that could be done. Sometimes one of us was able to slip away from the watchful guards under pretense of answering a call of nature and snap an overhead cable or roll a boulder onto a track to overturn a car.

Eventually we thought of a way both to sabotage and save ourselves work. We would leave the weakest at the foot of the log track to empty our boxes while the rest of us mined, broke coal, loaded the boxes and pushed them down the slippery logs. When no guard was around the lone man would drop trash, rocks, logs, bits of machinery, into the steel cars and cover them with coal. It did not take nearly so long to get out what looked like a full car — a fake thirty tons.

We were always wet and muddy underground. Water dripped from the roof. Puddles and muck were underfoot. One night I tried to drop a rock into a conveyor belt cogwheel. In the act I slipped. One of my fingers was caught and nearly cut off. I made my way up the winding trail as fast as I could, which was not fast, holding the wound with blood oozing between my fingers.

At the top was a Dutch doctor on regular duty. He was a good and intelligent old man. He wrapped rags around my hand and stopped the bleeding. I got a few kicks from a guard for not reporting to my foreman that I was injured and getting permission to go topside.

The Dutch doctor and I had long talks on our hikes between prison and mine. He was widely read, knew the ins and outs of European politics. He was strongly for a "United States of Europe." He had been captured in Java. He tried to learn to read English from me and I learned some Dutch from him.

My cut finger was not serious compared with the broken bones and cracked skulls that some men got. Often it required an hour for the Japs to get injured men to the surface, what with signing papers and going through the formalities. If the men could possibly make it they were required to walk out without help, or with one or two men supporting them. There was a fast cable car which could have been used to take men up, but its use was not permitted.

Worst of All Beatings

The summer weeks went on and on, with my group alternating between day and night shifts. It was on a day shift that the most serious incidents of imprisonment happened to me: an injury and a beating.

I was creeping through a narrow lateral in the mine, bent over with a heavy prop on my back, unable to see ahead. A Jap was hollering for me to hurry. My timber hit an old upright and props fell from the roof onto me. I was all but smashed to the ground. I had to let down and be crushed or hold the position, supporting an all but unbearable weight. The heaviest timber was across my shoulder.

Slow and confused Javanese slaves were right behind me. They did not know whether to render help or retreat and make room for me. With two Japs out in front of me cursing, I held up the load while I felt to see if my clothing were caught on any snag or projection. Convinced at last that I was not entangled in any way, I heaved up the weight and jumped from under. As I cleared them the timbers fell with a crash along with tons of loose overhead rocks and clay. The passage well filled. I never found out what happened to the Javanese behind me.

I dropped to the muddy ground. I was too weary and shaken to move. The Japs howled for me to help them clear the passage. I couldn't get up. My head swayed and drooped. I was completely exhausted.

A cruel army guard whom we called the Black Devil happened along at that moment on an inspection tour. The minor Nips told him what had happened, blaming me. The Black Devil turned on me, swinging a thick pole. He beat me on my bent, curving back. He used both hands. He beat until I thought his object was to kill me, beat me as I had never been beaten before, beat me until I suppose I ceased to stir. Perhaps he thought I was dead.

Another mine official had got wind of the incident and came up. I was barely able to turn my head and look up at him. He recognized me as having been one of the strongest workers. He spoke to a guard in my behalf. He touched me with his toe and told me to go topside and rest.

Every tiny section of my head, legs, back, chest and arms hurt as I slowly crawled up that twisting, torturous, muddy path. Now and then I got to my feet, took a few steps, and fell. It was another Death March. But at last somehow daylight began to glimmer ahead and finally I was out on the surface into sunshine, fresh air, a warm and beautiful world. I snatched and gulped water. Like a hurt dog I got out of sight, around a corner. I leaned against a wall and had no thoughts, but panted and stared at nothing.

After a time a passing Korean handed me a piece of raw onion. The sting of it in my mouth brought tears to my eyes and renewed the action of my mind. I lay down in the sunshine and rested. A thunder of planes in about midafternoon aroused me.

American planes, about three hundred, appeared. Those pilots may have had good luck charms and rabbit's feet and their guardian angels, but they will never know the praise and prayers I lifted for them as they sailed over in a steady stream that summer day. It was the largest flight of American machines I had ever seen in all my life. They spelled Invasion, Defeat and Freedom.

I Plan Escape

Fortunately the day following my clubbing was a *yasume** day. All prisoners were allowed to rest. I could not have worked anyhow. When I was sent back to work it was on night shift. I felt weaker and more despondent than I had ever felt in all my years. That night Bostic, Rebufatti, Dengelegi and I found some large wooden boxes to put in the steel cars and cover with coal, and we were allowed to go early to the surface by our surprised and pleased boss.

The next day Major McCarthy of the R.A.F., a fellow prisoner, brought me a week-old Japanese newspaper to decipher. He talked the Japs into letting me lay off that night. He told me that my back was bruised black and blue and yellow all over. There was no medicine of any sort. I lay and sat and stood, unable to be quiet because of the hurt, and deciphered the paper, thereby learning that the Nips had been wiped out at Okinawa.

We had half-suspected this owing to the fact that almost every hour of the day saw American bombers over the land. Once we had witnessed a dogfight between small planes right over our camp. It was only about 315 miles to the center of Okinawa and the Yanks were really keeping the air rails hot.

Through the request of Major McCarthy I was permitted to go out the next day with a group of crippled prisoners whom the Nips allowed to roam over the region under guard in search of frogs and water-snakes for soup meat. I had escape in mind now and wished to get the lay of the land so that I could travel at night. I felt that invasion was at hand. I longed to get away from the dreadful mines and meet the Yanks coming in. Besides, we prisoners had a feeling that when the invasion came we would all be slain by our captors for their own safety.

The following night I was sent back to the diggings. With Bostic

*Rest day for workmen.

and Rebufatti covering for me as honcho I returned to the surface and made my way to a vegetable garden I had spotted on the hike with the snake hunters. I got all the squashes I could carry, hid them, and returned to work. The little journey had been solely for the purpose of seeing if I could do it, in preparation for escape.

We threw many logs into the steel car that night so as to get away and eat the squash raw before it got light enough for the Japs to see us. We devoured them in a dark huddle and I ate so much that I could not sleep that day.

Atom Bomb

In the course of the sleepless forenoon I heard two crippled English prisoners discussing a huge dark cloud that could be seen against the sky off toward Nagasaki and Sasebo some thirty miles or so distant. I tossed in my opinion that I bet it was smoke from naval oil reservoirs at Sasebo that probably had been bombed when we heard a great rumbling a few minutes before.

In that bantering manner we passed off one of the world's great events. It was some time before we learned that the rumble and smoke had been caused by the world's second atomic bomb.

Americans Get the Fist

We should have known that something drastic had taken place, for soon after the Great Black Smoke, when news had time to get around, angry and excited Japanese began appearing everywhere, ordering prisoners to stand at attention and demanding to know their nationality. If the answer was American he got a fist to the jaw and a boot for the parade ground. There the camp commander kept us standing for hours, frequently waving his arms wildly and shouting at us: "You Americans! You beasts and murderers! You lie. You steal. You will not work hard. You eight Americans give us more trouble than all the other three hundred and twenty prisoners put together."

All he got for that was chuckles of appreciation.

"You are an evil race. You are unclean now from the sewers. You must cleanse yourselves. Ha, we shall cleanse you!"

Yeah, if we couldn't imagine an atomic bomb we knew there was something big. Invasion was the only thing we could think of. We believed it had started.

When he lined up all men guilty that day of various infractions he lightly slapped the British, Australians, Dutch and Javanese, but the American "guilties" were beaten horribly before our eyes, then were thrown into solitary confinement on half rations.

A Nip Gets Kicked

Our prison barracks were becoming so infested with lice and fleas that it was impossible to get a night's sleep. Forced to lie in such small space in the hot August weather, one would stick to the skin of a perspiring man on either side of him. We lived more like hogs at Fukuoka 27 than we had at Osaka, and were not fed enough to keep a pet poodle alive.

On the night of August 14, 1945, I was so weary and so tired of toiling for the Japs and being cursed and hollered at like a horse that I began shouting back at my boss in his own language. I finally told him he was a dirty turtle and he could go to the Japanese equivalent of hell, and sat down. He came at me with an axe. I sprang up and seized his arm. Dengelegi flew in and twisted the axe away from him. The Ainu and I fought with our fists. As puny as I was I knocked him down, for the Orientals don't understand fist-fighting and only those with the upper-class education and training have a knowledge of judo.

When he rose he was on the upgrade side of me, which gave him a distinct advantage. I kicked him between the legs below the stomach. It was enough for him. He went to his knees gasping and rasping for breath while he whined with pain. I fled, knowing that if I remained I would have to kill him, or more likely, that the guards would kill me. I got away. The day that dawned was one of suspense, as I expected every minute to be arrested and executed. However, losing a fight in Japan is a loss of face and a major disgrace in one's life. My kick had cooled the Ainu boss to the extent that he did not appear for work that night.

The Great News Breaks

The following day, August 16, when the daily crop of injured men was brought back to camp, the word was passed to me that the boss was waiting to kill me that night. A pleasant prospect. In my mind I planned to blow up the entire tunnel in the coal mine, leaving the Ainu trapped behind. I thought of other plans for protection also but this one seemed the safest.

About three o'clock that afternoon a strange change came over the camp. Jap guards came around and said there would be no more work. Messengers were sent to the mines, and after a while guards came marching the prisoners in. It was announced that the night shift would not work.

We couldn't guess what was happening. We were uneasy. We wondered if we were to be executed en masse. Some of the returning men told queer things. They had seen some Nips crying, and some praying. Then Nips told us the work had been stopped so that they could pray for the emperor. An idea popped up that the emperor was dead. Others thought it was the invasion.

I decided that our guessing was all wrong, when, in passing through the prison yard to find a clean rag for my injured finger, I passed a Jap guard and saluted. He did not return my salute but tucked his head and refused to notice me. Other guards I passed did the same thing. I thought they were ashamed of something. The death of the emperor or invasion would not make them ashamed. I knew them too well for that. I asked myself a breath-taking question — can it be the war is over and the Japs are licked?

That evening I cornered a guard and cross-examined him. Finally he talked. He said definitely that hostilities had ceased. We were given a little extra rice for our supper, and we demanded that the Nips give us our American and British Red Cross supplies which they had been hoarding in a warehouse for months or years. They reluctantly gave us the boxes and some medicine.

That night no prisoner slept. A few men got slapped by guards but there were definitely no serious beatings. All night we ate and sang and talked, and talked, and talked.

An Australian acquaintance, a man who had lived a rough life in

Hong Kong, Shanghai and Sydney as a gambler, beachcomber, drunkard and all-round incorrigible, came to me with a smile and extended hand.

"Mac," he said as we shook, "it almost makes me want to be a Christian."

CHAPTER VIII

Liberation

The very next day, August 17, 1945, we Americans were moved to a more comfortable prison camp about forty kilometers distant at a small coal mining city named Izzuka. The captain in charge growled at us when we refused to salute him but there were no beatings. After a week we were bored by idleness. The fickleness of humanity! We had been wanting rest. However, we had been expecting daily to see columns of Allied troops coming over the hills. The suspense was getting us down.

Early one morning, though something happened at last. We heard a roar, then saw a big B-29 coming in.[1] It circled lower and lower over our camp until we were able to make out words on the under-wing: "Prisoner of War Supplies." Immediately, small burdened parachutes were dropped. We prisoners yelled and scattered like quail, running, reaching up, trying to meet them halfway.

These 'chutes were nothing less than angels. They brought us food, clothing and medicines from heaven. We collected the stuff in the prison yard and divided it. I got two cans of peaches and a can of corned beef and they were good to the last lick and crumb. For dessert I had a can of peanuts and two chocolate bars.

The following day more bombers came over, dropping more food and clothing and three copies of a day-old Honolulu newspaper. Representatives of the Swiss and Swedish legations from Tokyo had already told us about the atomic bombs. We hadn't thought much about them, supposing them to be just another development of high explosive, perhaps a bit different from the usual, but here were papers running over with stories about the atomic bombs and many details about the Jap surrender.

We Take Our Freedom

After reading the papers we decided to liberate ourselves without waiting for the Yanks. The Nip commander objected to letting us outside the walls even to go walking and sightseeing. We told him that if he did not let us go, MacArthur would likely have all the Japs connected with the prison lined up against their own walls and shot. That melted him but he warned us that the war might start again as no terms had been settled upon. We said that didn't worry us. He offered to send along guards to protect us. We declined with Bronx cheers.

As we bulged into Izzuka town we met crowds of idle, silent, staring and puzzled Japanese. One old woman turned her head at the sight of us and wept.

A Jap miner carelessly-on-purpose bumped into me and knocked me from the narrow sidewalk. I seized his collar, doubled my fist and ordered him to attention. As he stood stiff I slapped his face, there before his countrymen. What a satisfying smack it was. I ignored the Jap people from then on. I suppose I strutted. I guess I acted like the classic conqueror. I went where I wished, inspected what I desired to see. I wasn't the only one; I suppose most of the Yanks were doing about the same thing.

Early in our freedom some of us came upon a drama with Chinese and Japanese as the actors. Chinese from a nearby concentration camp had rounded up about forty Japs and were preparing to hang them. Already they had several strung up by the feet to an overhead waterline. On the side opposite the Chinese was a big bunch of Jap soldiers with rifles, threatening to shoot. Both races turned to us onlookers to handle the trouble. They appealed solely to us Americans, ignoring white men of other nations. Skinny, sickly Americans called on by the erstwhile mighty Nips! We ordered the Chinese to let the Japs down and for both sides to disperse. This might look like coddling the Japs and ignoring the Good Neighbor policy toward the Chinese, but I think the truth was that we were trying to prevent trouble starting up by hundreds of wandering armed Japs against unarmed prisoners. Our orders were obeyed.

Little Tour of Japan

I decided to travel and see the land of cherry blossoms while waiting for our occupation forces to arrive. With the idea of locating old friends I entered the Jap commander's office to use his telephone. He offered to get my number and I told him I was getting my own numbers, roughly, like that! However, the operator refused to put through a long-distance call to the Fukuoka headquarters camp, so I went directly to the central telephone office. The operators were a little scared but I did some demanding and they soon had my number. I was able to talk with prisoners and discovered that friends were at Kokura only fifty kilometers away.

The train for Kokura was crowded with unarmed Jap soldiers and civilians, blank-faced and space-staring. I ordered the conductor to find a seat for me. He cleared two seats. He did not ask for a ticket. Just for the record I told him that all trains now belonged to MacArthur and what was MacArthur's was mine.

I spent two weeks traveling over Honshu Island, visiting camps where friends might be found. I went to a few old Japanese castles to learn something of the ancient Jap culture and architecture. The castles I saw showed about the same workmanship that prevailed in American pioneer log cabins and fortifications.

At Kyoto, near Osaka, which is supposedly the center of ancient Japanese culture,[2] I found that the geisha houses were cleaner and showed more skill in woodcarving and decorations than any other buildings. I walked right into the first geisha house in my new muddy G.I. shoes that had been dropped by the parachutes, making tracks on the clean grass mats. The girls screamed and motioned for me to remove my shoes. I grinned. A Jap military policeman was called. He took me for a news correspondent and explained that it was the custom in Japan to remove the shoes before entering a house. I told him in perfect sentences in his own language that I had been compelled to learn the customs of his land for the last three years and that now since the war was over he could learn mine. He started to grip my arm. I made a fist. The armed Jap turned off into another room, sat down, and held his head in his hands and stared at the floor, while I sat on a stairway and tried to tune up the two-stringed Jap ukuleles I had picked up.

I am sure my conduct was not unique. Hundreds of wandering Americans all over Japan were doing just about as they pleased.

And speaking of addressing the cop in his own tongue, I now had a fairly fluent command of the three principal dialects of Japan. By three,

I mean the one spoken by the coolies, the one used by the vast middle class, and the one used at court, or as they say in Japan, the Tokyo language. The first two I had picked up by association; the third, from a book I had studied through my imprisonment.

More Embarrassed Than Bathers

Back on the coal mines island I walked into two different Japanese public baths. The people offered me a seat and kept right on with their stripping and bathing — men, women and children together in the same vat, as naked as rocks. They were not at all embarrassed. I was.

While strolling one evening I was about to pass a short-legged Japanese lady dressed in the typical beautiful print kimono with silk bows and a parasol to match. She stopped, bowed, and in her tongue said, "Good evening, honorable soldier." I was so taken aback that I smiled and dipped the bow back to her. We mentioned the weather. We spoke of the war's end. It developed that we both loved peace. I remarked that life would take a lift in about a week when the occupation soldiers arrived. To my amazement, the lady broke into tears and sobs and finally asked me, "Is it true they will kill all but the prettiest girls? Will the prettiest girls not become slaves? Do you not think I am pretty?"

I hurried on.

I found that a good many Japanese really expected to be put to death by the American troops at sight. That was the result of vicious propaganda through the war years. I assured them that the Americans were better sports than their own soldiers and that only bad people would be killed.

Americans Have Everything

It was at Kokura, which was to have been the third atomic-bombed city, that I saw my first American soldiers from the new army. I say "new" because they were new to me from uniforms to helmets to firing equipment. I was to see things we early Yank soldiers had never dreamed of, such as K-rations, bazookas, WACS, WAVES and girl Marines. But this

first time it was about fifteen infantrymen and two officers in the liberation party. They flew into Japan something like two weeks ahead of the
main occupation force.

Among the Yanks in strange garb was a young sergeant of Japanese
descent. I saw the Japanese comparing the clean, neat soldiers to their
own sloppy, faded-out army men. Our fellows had large hunting
knives — maybe they were the army bolo — on their belts. One of the lieu-
tenants was a giant of a fellow. The Japs kept watching and sidling away
from him. Then they spied the American-Japanese sergeant, with every
eye focusing on the Nisei.

At first they could not grasp the anomaly. I heard talk among them,
how much the Americans had, plenty of food, new bright guns, worlds
of airplanes. Then an old woman barked hoarsely, "They've even got
Japanese soldiers!"

When the Nisei sergeant spoke up and warned them that no harm
must come to American prisoners, it was the last straw.

Nagasaki, the A-Bombed

The little liberation party had a radio and I listened to my first
American radio program since Bataan. They played a song entitled "Sentimental Journey." The Yanks assured us gathering prisoners that we
would be starting on that journey just as soon as they got our names and
serial numbers. I clipped my number off for them — 38012228 — and
made up my mind instantly that I'd seen enough of the slant-eyed kingdom and was going to take the journey home.

Back at Izzuka I had left a few personal possessions and some Japanese dolls that I had collected for people in the States. I decided the stuff
wasn't worth going after. All I wanted right then was to be on my way
to the land across the sea, more eager to see the strange new America
than anything else in Japan.

I boarded a train and went to Nagasaki. Despite my new hurry I
did take a look at the city's ruins. Ashes, charred bricks, twisted metal.
Around the edges of the blasted section, five or six or seven miles from
the center, every standing object slanted outward at a considerable angle,
even the trees. Away from the center some concrete and steel had with-

stood the blast somewhat, but all furniture, window frames, doors, and things of light metal were just ash. Yet it lacked what I had seen in shelled and bombed cities — great heartbreaking heaps of building rubbish and mangled bodies. I kept thinking that one instant live bodies had been walking about as people; the next instant they were not. But I still did not grasp the full significance of what I beheld, did not realize that at that moment most of the civilized world was thinking about this very small spot on the earth.

A Ride with Tommies

Allied ships were able to dock at Nagasaki despite damaged and crowded facilities. Some were taking away liberated prisoners. Our army, navy and Red Cross had established a clearing station. I stepped into line and presently was answering endless questions from curious Marines and sailors of a later vintage than myself. Since then I have answered thousands of questions, but it was on the docks of Nagasaki that I was asked, by an American woman, the only one that was really absurd.

"I suppose you have had oodles and oodles of rice," she said.

"Hell yes, more than I could eat," I yapped rudely, in astonishment.

"And always with plenty of cream and sugar, I suppose."

Curtains.

After a bath, new clothes and all the ice cream, ham sandwiches and cold fruit juices I wished, topped off with plenty of coffee and milk, I underwent medical inspection and was passed on to wait for transportation. I learned that only one ship was to leave right away.

McBride in a newspaper photograph with his medals after the war, around 1945.

It was the British aircraft carrier *Speaker*. My papers did not call for *Speaker* but I was in a rush. I got into a landing boat with a bunch of British people and presently was on the British ship and no objections made. My English cousins gave me courteous treatment and the first bed with a real mattress and sheets that I had enjoyed in years.

As we sailed out I did not look back. I had no regrets, and I seemed empty of all hate and thoughts of revenge. Perhaps I felt that the B-29's and the atom bombs had straightened things up for me.

One day put us on Okinawa. The only fresh meat on the island that day had been flown in—I was told—and liberated prisoners had the priority on it. Pork chops! The first fried meat I had in more than three years. As I was doing the chow line shuffle up to the savory odors, a hand smashed down on my shoulder.

"Hi, Mac!" said a voice. You remember that jerky you gave me on the way to Camp O'Donnell? I'll bet those pork chops won't taste any better than that jerky."

It was that Texas A&M college man, John Moseley of Quanah, Texas. He had come down from Manchuria, and he said, when we had eaten, "You guys in Japan sure had it cushy, from what we heard up north—free to run around the cities as you liked, going to movies and restaurants and not working much. Some people have all the luck." I grinned. How stories out of whole cloth do get around in the army!

On to Manila

Hearing that we might have to wait on Okinawa two days or more for a ship to Manila, a half a dozen of us got to sniffing around and picked up wind that a plane was to leave that night. We took a truck and went to the field. A big C-47 lay there. The crew was resting or asleep. One of them saw us and called. "Hi, where you Joes going?"

"Manila!" we yelped together, and were told to get aboard.

That moonlight voyage in the sky was great. I had left the Philippines as a slave in a prison ship; I was returning a free man. I sat in a seat with the radio operator. We watched the radar screen. I told him about the radar apparatus we had in the Battle of Bataan. He was interested by my Philippine experiences. The plane's course was altered so that we flew over some of the towns of North Luzon. I looked down at towns I had known. It was a great trip.

The next day, all decked out in a new and up-to-date American uniform, with money in my pocket and ribbons on my chest — I had to ask what they all meant — I went to the Red Cross post office and asked for mail. I was handed my first long letter in three years from America. Also there were letters from old Filipino friends who had written just in hopes I would get back and receive them. As I read avidly a Red Cross girl walked up with a young woman in tow, who had come along with her letter, no other than my good friend Miss Rosalina Flores, who had picked the shrapnel from my leg. I forgot all about the American girls back in the States with the Chi Omega sorority at the University of New Mexico. I grabbed Rosalina and gave her a big hug and kiss. Maybe I was a little red in the face from the jeers and whistles of envious G.I.'s taking in the free show, but I recovered and presented Rosalina as "the best girl in the world."

Shortly afterward a group of us ex–POW's saw a number of young women nearby.

"Red Cross girls," said one of the men.

"No they ain't neither," said another. "Look, one of 'em had sergeant's stripes."

"My Gawd, have they got wimmen in the army?"

"She's lookin' this way."

"Let's fade."

Trying to avoid some indefinite catastrophe in that direction, we all but bumped into some kind of a spick-and-span navy person. A woman. Young, good looking. We gaped, not knowing whether to salute, flirt, or run. This strange new America! She gave us a flashing smile, probably realizing we were just a bunch of dumb ex–POW's.

V for Victory Pants

I hadn't forgotten the promise to Miss Josephine Salanga who had made the shorts for me at San Fernando with the colored V. They were pretty well worn by now, but I donned them for a march in Manila. With them I wore wood-soled sandals and an old straw hat. Filipino and American friends went along. We were the focal point of many curious stares from the staid, young New Yanks in their stiff khaki, but we, or I, were excused by the MP's as we paraded along. I didn't know it then but an order had been given that all liberated Americans were not to be touched by the military police for any offense whatsoever.

"Oh, they're just some of the Bataan prisoners back from Japan. Half Filipino and half American — Filamericans they call 'em. Nuts, let 'em be."

"Look at the guy with the V on his pants."

"Yeah, prob'ly a patch, or he thinks it's cute."

Manila had been shelled, bombed, burned and looted by the Japs until it was hardly recognizable. I was disappointed until I saw some of the old familiar places and discovered that the Filipinos were smiling again and rebuilding their city.

Debris was being cleared away and new structures were under way in September 1945, and the world seemed happy. The Filipinos, I thought, must truly love their Manila, for there was a spirit which said, "We'll rebuild, we'll make it finer than ever, it's the capital of our homeland." I love the Filipinos and Luzon. Outside of the United States I would rather live there than any other place on earth I have seen.

Resurrection of a Diary

In a boat I crossed Manila Bay to the old Cabcaben docks and airfield to see if I could locate the tree where I had buried my diary on that morning of awful surrender. The field was well encroached upon by the jungle. I stood looking momentarily at the spot where the bursting shell had put shrapnel in my leg. I stared at the hill where we newly taken prisoners had stood for hours under artillery fire. I looked to see if my canteen might still be on the beach — which was silly. I stood for a long time thinking of the start of the March of Death from a spot nearby. No other Americans were around me now. Suddenly the hot, still jungle was dreadfully silent and lonely. I spoke to the two Filipino youths with me and we hunted for my tree.

I found the right tree without difficulty. The boys cut brush and dug for me. Presently they turned up color. I finished the job carefully with my bolo. All I found was rust and mold. Four rainy seasons had done for my precious diary and other papers. Not a page, not a decipherable line, not one recognizable fragment remained. I noticed some other fresh diggings. I wondered if other men had recovered their possessions. I got to my feet and laughed.

"You are a very strange man, Joe," said one of the Filipinos. "You do not find your buried treasure but still you are happy."

Maybe I was, maybe I wasn't.

While in Manila I helped army authorities to locate about sixty graves of American dead. I got back to La Union province and received many heartwarming welcomes from former associates.

As I was in the act of boarding the ship for home, the transport USS *Tyron*, Filipino friends appeared on the dock with a little monkey dressed in a tiny Japanese soldier uniform.

"It is for you to show the people in America how we made monkeys out of the Japs," they said.

But the port authorities gave me the iron jaw — I could not take the little fellow on board without inspections and inoculations and formal papers. The ship was ready to turn loose from the dock.

As we sailed through Manila Bay I stood by the rail, with Manila vanishing and the Bataan peninsula growing larger on our right. The sun was setting and the sky was red. Bataan looked lonely, abandoned, empty. And I remembered my home, my people and many other things.

I think I must have spent half the voyage across the Pacific at the rail, gazing and thinking and wondering. As we sailed through the Golden Gate at San Francisco, under the great bridge and on, we passed Alcatraz Prison, "The Rock." Its painted buildings looked clean and secure and comfortable, with smoke rising warmingly. I muttered to one of the liberated men beside me, "God, if only we could have spent our four years in there!"

Chapter Notes

Chapter I

1. For an interesting account of the events just prior to the beginning of the march, the reader is referred to Carlos P. Romulo, *I Saw the Fall of the Philippines*, 1946, pp. 301–302.

2. Stephen M. Mellnik, "The Life and Death of the 200th Coast Artillery," *Coast Artillery Journal*, Vol. LXX (April 1947), pp. 2–7.

3. Dovis Hofmann, "Women in Philippine Life," *On to the Philippines*, Vol. I (October 1945), p. 23.

4. Joe Smith, "We Shoot Down the First Japs," *Life*, Vol. XXX (December 1941), p. 30.

5. Bert Silen, "Manila Broadcast," National Broadcasting Company, December 9, 1941.

6. Jonathan M. Wainwright, "This Is My Story," *Chicago Herald-American*, November 18, 1945, p. 7.

7. Amea Willoughby, *I Was on Corregidor*, 1943, p. 80.

8. Mellnik, *op. cit.*, p. 5.

9. Romulo, *op. cit.*, p. 59.

10. Mellnick, *op. cit.*, p. 5.

11. United Press, "Jap Aircraft Shot Down by Tiny Force," in *El Paso Herald-Post*, January 1942.

12. Mellnick, *op. cit.*, p. 6.

13. *Op. cit.*, p. 291

Chapter II

1. "The Philippines: 1942," *Time*, March 12, 1945, p. 6.

2. Ruth Benedict, *Chrysanthemum and the Sword*, 1946, pp. 20–42.

3. "General in Plea for Bataan Men," *The Albuquerque Tribune*, February 1948, p. 1.

4. Catherine Porter, *Crisis in the Philippines*, 1942, pp. 35–36.

Chapter III

1. F. S. Marquardt, *Before Bataan and After*, 1943, p. 25.

2. Ruth Benedict, *Chrysanthemum and the Sword*, 1946, pp. 20–42.

3. Letter from Major General J. A. Ulio, December 8, 1945, now in author's collection.

4. Catherine Porter, *Crisis in the Philippines*, 1942, p. 56.

5. Letter from Josephine Salanga, March 24, 1946, now in author's collection.

6. Robert B. Lapham, *Britannica Book of the Year*, 1946, pp. 358–360.

7. Letter from Josephine Salanga, September 25, 1945, in author's collection.

8. F. S. Marquardt, *Before Bataan and After*, 1943, p. 51.

9. Claire Phillips, "I Was an American Spy," *The Reader's Digest*, May 1945, p. 33.

Chapter IV

1. Alfred C. Oliver Jr., "I Saw This Happen," *Foreign Service*, Vol. XXXIV (January 1947), p. 18.

Chapter VI

1. Ruth Benedict, *Chrysanthemum and the Sword*, 1946, pp. 43–75.
2. John Bowen, "Patient Tells of Jap Brutality," *Camp Carson Mountaineer*, November 1945, p. 3.
3. Jonathan B. Wainwright, "This Is My Story." *Chicago Herald-American*, November 1945, p. 7.
4. Marion F. White, "Cry Havoc Performance Dedicated to Myrrl McBride," *Sul Ross Skyline*, Vol. XXI (May 1944), p.1.
5. Livingston P. Noell Jr. "My Japanese Jailer," *The Saturday Evening Post*, August 1945, pp. 3–4.

6. "The Tolerant Vanquished," *Newsweek*, September 1945, p. 33.
7. "Back from the Grave," *Time*, February 1945, pp. 13–14.
8. "The Cities Turn to Ashes," *Life*, May 1945, p. 56.
9. *Ibid.*, p. 57.

Chapter VIII

1. "Back from the Grave," *Time*, September 1945, p. 5.
2. N. Orui, *Castles in Japan*, 1935, p. 39.

Bibliography

Books

Benedict, Ruth. *Chrysanthemum and the Sword*. New York: Houghton Mifflin, 1947. This author was assigned by the Office of War Information to make a complete report on the Japanese from the standpoint of the anthropologist. This is an extensive and detailed analysis of the patterns of Japanese culture. It explains the unique behavior of the Nipponese in war.

Orui, N. *Castles in Japan*. Tokyo: Maruzen Co., Ltd., 1940. This book was designed to help tourists learn something about Japan's characteristic culture. It includes bibliographies which are apparently authoritative and reliable guides in study.

Marquardt, F. S. *Before Bataan and After*. New York: Reynal-Hitchcock, 1943. A former schoolteacher who worked on Luzon gives information concerning politics and education in the Philippines. The report praises the American colonial policy in the islands.

Porter, Catherine. *Crisis in the Philippines*. New York: Longmans Green, 1942. The author makes generalizations concerning the economic life of the Philippines. Accurate information regarding the various political factions and cultures is also included.

Romulo, Carlos P. *I Saw the Fall of the Philippines*. New York: Doubleday, 1946. An interesting book written by the former editor and publisher of a Philippine newspaper chain. Romulo's newspaper articles won the Pulitzer Prize for "better understanding between nations" in 1941. The editor gives a detailed account of the fall of the Philippines from material he kept in a personal diary. The story sounds over-dramatic in places but is for the most part a true and vivid account of the life on Luzon after the Japanese invasion. The author reflects the general attitude of the educated Filipino toward America and the war.

Willoughby, Amea. *I Was on Corregidor*. New York: Harper & Brothers, 1943. The wife of a politician and a leader in the gilded society of Manila gives her eyewitness account of the beginning of the war. The author does nothing heroic herself but makes no pretensions in this respect. Her stay on Corregidor ends when she is sent home on an American submarine.

Articles

"Back from the Grave," *Time*, September 1945. A summary of the liberation activities of American troops in Japan. The report deals with prominent Americans who were survivors of Japanese imprisonment.

Bowen, John. "Patient Tells of Jap Brutality," *Camp Carson Mountaineer*, November 1945. A liberated American soldier relates the horrible conditions at Yodogawa prison in Japan.

"The Cities Turn to Ashes," *Life*, May 1945. Pictures of the bombed-out sections of Japanese cities reveal the heavy toll taken by American bombers.

"General in Plea for Bataan Men," *The Albuquerque Tribune*, February 1948, p. 1.

Hofmann, Dovis. "Women in Philippine Life," *On to the Philippines*, October 1945. This small folder was prepared in Australia as a guide for Allied soldiers who were on their way for invasion and recapture of the Philippines. The folder contains several sections dedicated to such subjects as language, customs, history and geography of the Philippines.

Lapham, Robert B. "Guerrilla Warfare," *Britannica Book of the Year*, 1946. An army colonel who was with the guerrillas in the Philippines gives brief information concerning the size, operations, and organization of underground activities in the Philippine Islands.

Lee, Henry G. "Man of Bataan's Legacy to His Country," *Saturday Evening Post*, Vol. XXI (June 1946). These poems were selected by the *Saturday Evening Post* editors as the best written by a soldier in World War II.

Mellnik, Stephen M. "The Life and Death of the 200th C.A. (AA)," *Coast Artillery Journal*, Vol. LXX (April 1947). A complete history of the 200th Coast Artillery regiment is reported by a colonel who experienced the fighting, suffering and persecution of the group.

Noell, Livingston P. "My Japanese Jailer," *Saturday Evening Post*, August 1945. An American doctor relates his experiences with a typical Japanese officer commanding a work detail of Allied prisoners of war.

Oliver, Alfred C. "I Saw This Happen," *Foreign Service*, Vol. XXXIV (January 1947). An unbiased account of life at Cabanatuan prison. The author reports many instances of Japanese torture.

"The Philippines: 1942," *Time*, March 12, 1945, p. 6.

Phillips, Claire. "I Was an American Spy," *Reader's Digest*, May 1945. The personal narrative of an American adventuress who remained loyal to her country and gathered intelligence information for guerrilla leaders.

Smith, Joe. "We Shoot Down the First Japs," *Life*, Vol. XXX (December 1941). Pictures and reports from two Americans who fired an anti-aircraft gun at the Japanese bombers during the first attack on Luzon.

"The Tolerant Vanquished," *Newsweek*, September 1945. This report describes the attitude of the Japanese press toward defeat and surrender.

United Press. "Jap Aircraft Shot Down by Tiny Force," *El Paso Herald-Post*, January 1942.

Wainwright, Jonathan M. "This Is My Story," *Chicago Herald-American*, November 18, 1945. The personal narrative of the general who surrendered himself and the Philippine Islands to the Japanese. He gives an accurate picture of some of the phases of Japanese brutality.

White, Marion F. "Cry Havoc Performance Dedicated to Myrrl McBride," *Sul Ross Skyline*, Vol. XXI (May 1944). A conventional news story.

Wolfert, Ira C. "Lest We Forget," *Reader's Digest*, April 1945. The author describes his voyage on a Japanese hell ship. His experience was similar to that of thousands of other Allied prisoners who were captured by the Japanese.

Letters

Salanga, Josephine. letter, September 25, 1945, in author's collection.

Salanga, Josephine. letter, March 24, 1946, in author's collection.

Ulio, J. W. letter, December 8, 1945, in author's collection.

Other Sources

Silen, Bert. "Manila Broadcast," National Broadcasting Company, December 9, 1941.

Index

201